Judaism in a Nutshell

An Easy-to-Use Guide
For People Who Are Long on Curiosity,
But Short on Time.

Passover

Shimon Apisdorf

Judaism in a Nutshell: Passover
by Shimon Apisdorf

Copyright © 2003 Shimon Apisdorf

ISBN 1-881927-28-8

Cover design by Staiman Design
Page layout by Zisi Berkowitz
Editing and proofing by Sharon Goldinger, Nachum Shapiro
and Hadassa Goldsmith

**Distributed to the trade by Biblio: www.bibliodistribution.com
Distributed to Judaica stores by Judaica Press: (800) 972-6201 or
www.judaicapress.com**

All books from Leviathan Press are available at bulk order
discounts for educational, promotional and fund-raising purposes.
For information call (800) 538-4284.

Printed in the United States of America

ACKNOWLEDGEMENTS

Rabbi Michel and Rebbetzin Feige Twerski, Rabbi Menachem Goldberger, Bill Hackney, Andrea Schulman, Aryeh Mezei, Nachum (the Enforcer) Shapiro, Hillel Soclof, Sanford & Eppie Shore, Avi Weinstein, Itchie Lowenbraun, Rabbi Asher Resnick, Camille & Shirley, and Fred Rosenberg

SPECIAL THANKS

My parents, David and Bernice Apisdorf
Mr. and Mrs. Robert and Charlotte Rothenburg
Esther Rivka, Ditzah Leah, Yitzchak Ben Zion, and Baruch Chananya—there is nothing like Passover with the four of you.
Miriam. You've done it again. You are an inspiration, and absolutely the perfect partner for walking, editing, coffee, learning, laughing and life.
Hakadosh Baruch Hu, source of all blessing

DEDICATION

This book is dedicated to my friend and colleague, Yigal Segal, a paragon of integrity, tireless work, and selfless dedication to *Klal Yisroel*. May you and your wife have only *nachas* from your beautiful family.

In Memoriam
This book is dedicated to the memory of Rivka Resnick.

PASSOVER IN A NUTSHELL is the fourth volume in the
JUDAISM IN A NUTSHELL COLLECTION
Judaism in a Nutshell is one of many innovative, educational projects made possible by the Jewish Literacy Foundation

Jewish Literacy Foundation

17 WARREN ROAD, SUITE 18
(410) 602-1020
WWW.JEWISHLITERACY.ORG

PIKESVILLE, MD 21208
1-877-J-LITERACY
INFO@JEWISHLITERACY.ORG

table of *contents*

introduction

Take Me Out to the Seder, Take Me Out to the Game

My wife and I go with our children to baseball games, I went with my father to baseball games, and my father went with his father to baseball games, but that's as far back as the chain stretches. On the other hand, every year my wife and I have a Passover seder with our children, we had a seder with our parents, our parents had a seder with their parents, their parents had a seder with their parents, and on and on and on.

The Passover experience is a living chain that stretches *waaay* back—back before the days of Sandy Koufax, Ty Cobb, and Abner Doubleday (the inventor of baseball), before Benjamin Franklin, Napoleon Bonaparte, Ferdinand and Isabella, Richard the Lion Hearted, Saladin, Mohammed, Paul, Julius Caesar, Plato, Confucius, Buddha, Homer, and just about anyone else you can think of.

Now, to be perfectly honest, many people have a problem with Passover. In fact, their problem with Passover is indicative of a problem that lots of people have with Judaism in general. People think that since Judaism stretches so *waaay* back it must also be *waaay* out of touch with the real world they live in.

Well, I'm here to tell you that Passover, and Judaism, are actually much more in touch than most people realize. The truth is, I grew up thinking that Passover was little more than a bunch of musty old rituals that for some reason you *had* to do every year with your family, whether you liked it or not. And that's basically what I thought about Judaism, too.

Don't get me wrong—I was always proud to be a Jew. I always felt a special connection when I was with other Jews. But when it came to the religious stuff, well, it was just so old. Quaint, perhaps, but very, very old, and therefore it seemed very, very outdated. Judaism may have been warm and fuzzy in that cultural roots sort of way, but it was clearly *waaay* irrelevant to real life.

My Life Story, at Least so Far

At this point, what you know about me is that I like baseball, I grew up not knowing what to make of Judaism, I'm now married with kids, we have a family seder every Passover, and I'm the author of the book you are holding. Frankly, if you want more details—especially the embarrassing ones—you'll just have to ask my wife. For now, the only other thing I'm going to reveal is that I am thoroughly in love with Passover. To me, Passover has become an absolute highlight of the year—kind of like the World Series, only bigger. And now you know one more thing. You know *why* I wrote this book. This book is for people who think that at best Passover is a cozy, cultural family get-together, and at worst is so *waaay* out of touch that it doesn't matter if we lose touch altogether.

I wrote this book, as well as *The Survival Kit Family Haggadah*, because over the years I have found Passover to be astonishingly *in* touch with so many of life's most important issues. At one time or another (usually with a close friend or someone we love very much), we all find ourselves pondering the great issues of life. Issues like: meaning, purpose, spirituality, goals, dreams, freedom, family and love—the real issues of life. This may sound almost unbelievable, but Passover addresses a lot of those issues, and it has some fantastic things to say about them.

Few of the ideas contained in this book are novel. They are a bit of what I have discovered so far, refracted through the lens of this baseball-loving American Jew's attempt to live a thoughtful and spiritually vibrant life. It is my deepest hope that through these pages you, too, will discover that there just may be far more to Passover, and to life, than you ever imagined. By the way, if you happen to be in Baltimore this spring, consider yourself invited to our seder. And who knows, maybe we'll even go to a ball game together.

Passover: what's the big *Deal?*

1

Passover is both the first and last Jewish holiday. It's the first holiday because it was the very first holiday that God instructed the Jews to celebrate. It is also the last holiday because time and again demographic studies of the Jewish community show that Passover is the most widely observed of all the holidays. In other words, while many Jews may opt out of *Sukkot* because they don't have a clue of what it's about, *Shavuot* because they have never heard of it, or *Rosh Hashanah* because it's boring or conflicts with an important business meeting, Passover is invariably the holiday that most Jews participate in. The question is why? Why did God choose Passover to be the very first holiday the Jews ever celebrated, and why is it that Jews find Passover so difficult to leave by the wayside?

The Mother of All Holidays

Big things happen in the course of your life. Marriage is big, your team winning the Super Bowl is big, college graduation is big, and having a child is big, but nothing is as big as your own birth. The most dramatic event in a person's life is the one that no one remembers; it's the experience of birth. Imagine if somehow we possessed *in utero* consciousness, and could remember what it was like to grow and develop in the womb and what it felt like when we actually made our dramatic entrance into the outside world. Now *that* would be really big.

The holiday of Passover marks the epic, seminal event of the Exodus of the Jewish people after centuries of slavery in Egypt. In the life of the Jewish people, Passover is the holiday that marks the birth of our nation, and that's big—really big. In a sense, all of Jewish history that preceded the Exodus was *in utero*, a period of pre-birth development, and everything that follows the Exodus is one long unfolding saga that could be titled *The Life and Times of the Jewish People*.

Let's take a moment to look at the main events in Jewish history so that we see precisely where Passover fits in.

OVERVIEW
EARLY JEWISH HISTORY, THE EXODUS, AND BEYOND

Birth of Abraham. . . . . 1812 BCE	Death of Moses . . . . 1272 BCE
Birth of Sarah. . . . . 1802 BCE	Joshua leads people into Israel. 1272 BCE
Covenant. God promises Abraham	David becomes King. . . . . 877 BCE
the land of Israel and tells him his	Jerusalem becomes capitol . . . . . 868 BCE
descendants will be slaves . . . 1742 BCE	First Temple built . . . . 825 BCE
Birth of Isaac . . . . 1712 BCE	First Temple destroyed;
Near sacrifice of Isaac . . . . 1675 BCE	Babylonian exile begins . . . . . . 422 BCE
Birth of Jacob and Esau. . . . . . . 1652 BCE	Purim events. . . . . 355 BCE
Sale of Joseph by brothers . . . . 1544 BCE	Second Temple built. . . . . 352 BCE
Joseph interprets dreams, becomes	Miracle of Chanukah . . . . 165 BCE
Prime Minister of Egypt . . . . . . 1531 BCE	Second Temple destroyed; Roman
Jacob, brothers of Joseph, and	exile begins . . . . 70 **CE**
families emigrate to Egypt . . . 1522 BCE	Babylonian Talmud compiled 500
Egyptian slavery begins. . . . . . 1428 BCE	First Crusade. 1096
Birth of Moses . . . . 1392 BCE	Holocaust 1939
Ten plagues, first Passover,	Rebirth of Israel 1948
and Exodus . . . . 1312 BCE	Reunification of Jerusalem. 1967
Torah given on Sinai, and building	Mass exodus of Russian Jews
of golden calf . . . . 1312 BCE	to Israel begins 1990
Second set of tablets given to	
Moses on Sinai. . . . . 1311 BCE	

Early Jewish History in a Nutshell:
It All Starts with Abraham

Abraham was a remarkable human being who became the founding father of a remarkable nation. Abraham lived in a world where dictatorship was the only known form of government, where the value of human life was an unheard of concept, where everyone believed that all events were a matter of fate, and where everyone thought that the sun, the clouds, and even sheep were gods that possessed great powers and were deserving of ultimate devotion. What made Abraham so remarkable is that, *on his own*, he arrived at a totally different understanding of reality than everyone else. Abraham's radical break with the rest of the planet can be summed up in one word—God. Beyond his unique ability to draw independent conclusions about life, Abraham's greatness expressed itself in his desire to share his enlightened thinking with the rest of the world as well. And so Abraham became the first person in history with a mission, a mission to change the world.

God is Tickled Pink

When God saw that at long last there was someone in the world who correctly understood what life was all about—and who was prepared to do something about it—He just couldn't contain Himself and immediately decided to have a talk with Abraham. This is how their conversation began—

> *"And God said to Abraham, 'Go out on your own; leave your land, the place of your birth, and your father's house and go to the land that I will show you. And I will make of you a great nation, and I will bless you and make you renowned; and you will be a source of blessing. I will bless those that bless you, and curse those that curse you, and all the families of the earth will be blessed through you.'...And Abraham took his wife Sarah and his nephew Lot, and all of their belongings, and all of the people who*

*they had influenced in Haran and they left for the land of
Canaan, and arrived in the land of Canaan.... And God
appeared to Abraham and said, 'I will give this land to
your descendants.'"*

Genesis 12:1-7

Not long after their first meeting, in the year 1742 BCE, God
and Abraham cut a deal known as the Covenant. As a part of this
Covenant, God promised Abraham that He would have a unique
relationship with his descendants, that they would grow into a
nation that would be a source of blessing for all mankind, and
that their place of residence would be a slice of the Middle East
called Israel. In a sense, the initiation of the relationship between
God and Abraham was the moment the Jewish people were
conceived.   It would still be another 350 years until the
descendants of Abraham would grow into a nation, but with the
Covenant between God and Abraham, the process of
development had begun. In the context of the Covenant,
Abraham was also informed that the final stage of the formative
period would be an experience of collective hardship.

*"And He [God] said to Abraham, 'You need to know that
your descendants will be strangers in a land that is not
theirs; and they will be enslaved and oppressed for four
hundred years. Eventually, however, I will judge the
nation that oppresses them, and then they will leave with
great wealth.'"*

Genesis 15:13-14

These words foreshadowed the labor-pain-like events that
would culminate in the Exodus—the birth of the Jewish nation—
and ultimately lead to the holiday of Passover.

From Abraham to Exodus:
When a Family Became a People

Here are the highlights of what happened to Abraham and

Sarah, their children and their grandchildren, and how they eventually showed up on the world scene as the nation of Israel. The story goes like this:

Abraham had a son named Isaac, Isaac had a son named Jacob, and Jacob had twelve sons (the twelve tribes of Israel), one of whom was Joseph. Joseph and his brothers didn't exactly see eye to eye; and their uneasy relationship imploded when the brothers sold Joseph to a caravan of merchants headed for Egypt and then told their father that he had been killed by a wild animal. Well, a funny thing happened to Joseph in Egypt. Thanks to a peculiar gift Joseph had for interpreting dreams, he was eventually appointed to be the Egyptian Prime Minister and right-hand man to Pharaoh himself.

Years after Joseph was sold by his brothers, a devastating famine hit the land of Israel (then known as Canaan), where Jacob, his sons, and their families lived. As luck would have it— based on his interpretation of one of Pharaoh's dreams—the new Prime Minister of Egypt had actually foretold the coming of this very famine. As a result, under Joseph's leadership, Egypt had stockpiled plenty of food and was capable not only of providing for itself but also of selling surplus grain to others.

Jacob heard about the grain that was being sold in Egypt and dispatched his sons to make a purchase. And guess who they had to meet with in order to purchase the food they needed? Their brother Joseph! Before long, Jacob was reunited with his long lost son, and the entire family relocated to the Egyptian suburb of Goshen. After a brief honeymoon period, the Egyptians turned on the Jews, and soon a new Pharaoh raised the specter of dual loyalty. Within a short period of time, the Jews were reduced to being brutally oppressed slave laborers.

Moses to the Rescue

While the Jews were suffering under the yoke of slavery, a Jewish baby by the name of Moses happened to be found and adopted by none other than the daughter of Pharaoh himself. After being raised in the palace of Pharaoh and witnessing the hardships imposed upon the people of his birth, Moses decided to cast his lot with the Jews. Once again, God was just delighted and some time later scheduled a meeting with Moses at the local burning bush. At that meeting, God introduced Himself as the God of Abraham, Isaac, and Jacob and told Moses that the Jews were His nation. God went on to inform Moses that the time of liberation had arrived and that Moses himself would be the one to negotiate with Pharaoh and lead the Jewish people to the land of Israel. All of that was a bit more than Moses had in mind when he decided to set out on a search for his Jewish roots, but when God says you're hired—you're hired.

As you can imagine, Pharaoh wasn't particularly enamored of his Jewish interlocutor, so God had to intervene a bit. Ten plagues later, Pharaoh threw open the gates of Egypt and the Jewish people were free.

Pass the Matzah, Easy on the Horseradish

The Jews who originally settled in Egypt were the grandchildren, great-grandchildren, and great-great-grandchildren of Abraham and Sarah; they were a family. With the Exodus from Egypt, while they were still a family—the "children of Israel"—they were also a free and independent nation. The story that began with Abraham and a Covenant led to the events surrounding Jacob and his children. The story of Jacob's sons, Joseph and his brothers, evolved into the story of the bondage in Egypt and Moses' mission of redemption, a story that culminated with the birth of the Jewish people.

The Exodus took place on the fifteenth day of the Hebrew month of *Nisan*, and has been commemorated ever since at the Passover seder. The Passover seder, with its matzah, four cups of wine, horseradish, and reading of the Haggadah, is the central element of the Passover holiday, and the way that Jewish families have been recounting, and reliving, the events of the Exodus for the last three thousand years.

In a sense, Passover is an attempt to re-experience birth itself—the birth of the Jewish nation.

Is the Seder Up to the Task?

Before we go on with an exploration of the whats, the hows, and the whys of Passover, it's important that we first reflect on a quote from the text of the Haggadah, a quote that carries with it one of the most remarkable notions in all of Judaism.

> *"In every generation, each and every person must see himself as though he personally experienced the Exodus from Egypt."*
>
> Text of the Haggadah

The notion that all Jews should see themselves as if they personally left Egypt is both perplexing and extraordinary. It's perplexing because, frankly, it just doesn't seem possible. I remember when the movie *Saving Private Ryan* came out and my sister warned me not to see it. She said that the images were so riveting and so disturbing that she couldn't sleep for three nights. A few years later, I watched maybe forty minutes of the film on video, and she was right. I tossed and turned all night. The scenes were so vivid that my body tingled as if I were actually experiencing the horrors of war—which of course I wasn't. So thanks to the cinematographic genius of Steven Spielberg, we can all be thrust back half a century and get an inkling of the utter horror that was World War II. Perhaps, just perhaps, Mr. Spielberg could do the same for the Exodus from Egypt (*The Prince of Egypt* just didn't do it for me), but short of a new blockbuster, it's hard to imagine that your average seder table at grandma's house can be transformed into a scene so alive with drama that people could actually see themselves as though they personally experienced the Exodus from Egypt. So what's the deal?

Cellular Jews

Consider the following: Everything that makes up your body—from the freckle on your nose to the chambers of your heart—is made up of cells. Most of these cells regularly reproduce themselves and are replaced throughout the course of your life. (I have a theory that all human itching can be traced to mitotic cell reproduction, but I'm not yet ready to publish it.) If you think about cell reproduction, what you will realize is that most of the cells you were born with are no longer with you, which raises the question—if most of my body has been reproduced, recycled, and replaced since I was born, am I still the same person who emerged from my mother's womb, or am I somebody else? The answer is, of course you are the same person; only the cells have changed.

The same is true with the Jewish people: The same Jewish nation that was born in Egypt is still with us today; only the cells have changed. Just like a human being can be considered from two perspectives—from a macro-global perspective, or from a micro-cellular perspective—the same is true of the Jewish people. You could say that, on the one hand, the Jewish people *is*, while, simultaneously, the Jewish people *are*. On the macro-global level, the Jewish people *is* a singular, spiritual-historical entity—a nation whose essence is its Covenant with God and whose entire existence is the unfolding dynamic of that Covenant. At the same time, the Jewish people *are* the millions and millions of Jews who reproduce and are replaced throughout history, yet nonetheless make distinct and unique contributions to the overall well-being of the nation.

Now, let's take this one step further. Within every cell is an acid called DNA, and within DNA is all of the information necessary to produce not just another cell but the entire person that cell is a part of. So, while bodies are made up of cells, cells themselves contain the essence of the entire body, and something similar can be said about the Jewish people. While the Jewish people may be made up of many Jews, within each and every Jew there lies the essence of the Jewish people—which brings us to the Jewish soul, and to the Haggadah.

The Ageless Wonder

I'd like to suggest that what the Haggadah is asking of us when it insists that *we see ourselves as if we personally experienced the Exodus from Egypt* has more to do with accessing a personal, inner dimension of ourselves than it does with recreating external, lifelike scenes of the Exodus. We all know that every human life, regardless of how vigorous and long lasting it may be, is ultimately fleeting and temporary. As Jews, however, an aspect of our existence transcends the ephemeral. At the Passover seder, all Jews are called upon to see their lives in the context of a larger, eternal reality to which they belong—that of the Jewish nation. Jews may get old and tired, but the Jewish nation—though born over three millennia ago—is mankind's ageless wonder.

> *"The Egyptian, the Babylonian, and the Persian rose, filled the planet with sound and splendor, then faded to dream-stuff and passed away. The Greek and the Roman followed, made a vast noise and they are gone. Other peoples have sprung up and held their torch high for a time, but it burned out, and they sit in twilight now, or have vanished. The Jew saw them all, beat them all, and is now what he always was, exhibiting no decadence, no infirmities of age, no weakening of his parts, no slowing of his energies, no dulling of his alert and aggressive mind. All things are mortal but the Jew. All other forces pass, but he remains."*
>
> Mark Twain

To Birth and Back Again

Think about this: Every senior citizen's dream come true would be the ability to "do it all over again," only this time with the wisdom of hindsight. That, in essence, is the opportunity the Haggadah lays before us. When the Exodus took place a little over 3,300 years ago, a people was born, and today that same people, that same nation of Israel, is still alive and well. At the same time, it's critical to remember that while each and every one of us is a cell in the great collective of the Jewish people, we are not *just* cells. Just like human beings go through stages of life and grow, develop, and adapt, similarly the Jewish nation, as it navigates its way through history, must continually draw on an array of inner resources to meet the challenges of life. And each and every one of us—each Jew in his or her own way—represents a unique resource for the Jewish nation, with the potential to offer a unique and deeply meaningful contribution to the life of the Jewish people.

So at the seder we try to connect with our essence, our soul—the part of us that possesses a transcendent bond with all Jews, and with the Jewish nation. It is from that place that we try to sense and imagine and feel the moment of collective epiphany known as the Exodus. We see a newly born nation liberated from bondage, driven by its Covenant, and boldly striding into the future. And then, simultaneously, we see ourselves as part of that very same vibrant people as it continues its odyssey through time.

The Jewish people may have been born over three millennia ago, but every year at Passover it is as if we are three thousand years young. Each Passover is an opportunity to begin our journey through history with the same inspired vitality that carried us out of Egypt; only now, we have the benefit of three thousand years of gathered wisdom.

all that Passover stuff:
a handy-dandy
Glossary

2

The holiday of Passover is the most intricate and multifaceted of all Jewish holidays. *Rosh Hashanah* has the *shofar* and synagogue services, and that's about it. *Chanukah* has the lighting of the *menorah*, and all *Yom Kippur* has is fasting and a bunch of prayers. Passover, however, is brimming with all sorts of stuff—from matzah, bitter herbs, and a game of hide-and-seek known as *afikomen*, to a special pre-Passover house cleaning, Passover dishes, even Passover ketchup, four sons, four questions, four cups of wine, and lots more. For this reason, I have chosen to provide here a glossary of Passover terms. That way, before we get into the nitty-gritty of the holiday, you can gain a basic familiarity with just about anything you may encounter related to Passover and any terms that will be used later in this book will already be familiar to you—or at least you will have somewhere to refer back to. So, here goes.

(By the way, if you just want to skim the glossary or even skip it altogether, that's okay. The rest of the book is not dependent on reading the glossary, and if you do run into words or terms you don't understand, you can always flip back to the glossary.)

Afikomen. The *afikomen* is a piece of matzah that is eaten near the end of the seder. When the Temple stood in Jerusalem, families would have a Passover lamb that was eaten at their seder. Today, in place of that lamb meat, we eat the *afikomen* as a reminder of how things were and how we hope they will be again one day. *See* matzah, Passover lamb.

Afikomen presents. These are gifts awarded to the child who finds the hidden *afikomen*. It is certainly appropriate for gifts to be given not only for finding the afikomen but also for trying to find the afikomen. That way, everyone is a winner. *See* afikomen, hiding and finding the afikomen.

Bedikat chametz. This is the Hebrew term for the final checking of the home for *chametz*. *See* Searching for chametz.

Bread of affliction. In the Torah (the Biblical five books of Moses), matzah is referred to as "bread of affliction." This is because matzah was a staple of the Jewish diet when the Jews were slaves. The Egyptians made the Jews subsist on matzah because it is filling and hard to digest and therefore they could be given less to eat. *See* matzah.

"Bringing up the dishes." Families that own separate sets of Passover dishes and utensils generally have a storage space where they are kept throughout the year, often in a basement. Thus, the term "bringing up the dishes" means *up* from the basement.

Burning chametz. On the morning before Passover begins, any *chametz* that was found during the search, or any remaining *chametz*, is burned. This burning is the final step in removing *chametz* from the home. Once the burning is done, the home is completely ready for Passover. *See* chametz.

Chad Gad'yah. After the conclusion of the seder, an epilogue of sorts consists of singing a number of songs that are unique to the seder night. One of the most famous of these songs is *Chad Gad'yah*, which is Aramaic for "one young goat." This song is about the seemingly futile nature of life if not for the presence of a Divine reality. *See* seder.

Chametz. *Chametz* is the generic term for all types of leaven or fermented grain products that one may not eat, own, or benefit from on Passover.

Charlton Heston. Charlton Heston starred as Moses in the classic Hollywood film *The Ten Commandments*. Heston was a pretty good casting choice for Moses, but Edward G. Robinson as Pharaoh was a real stretch.

Charoses. *Charoses* is a mixture of ground nuts, chopped apples, wine, and cinnamon, though there are variations on the ingredients. One of the symbolic elements on the seder plate, it is a pasty substance that symbolizes the mortar used by the Jews in their slave labor projects in Egypt. *See* seder plate.

Chatzot. *Chatzot* is the Hebrew word for midnight. According to Jewish law, it is preferable that the *afikomen* at the end of the seder be eaten before midnight. (The Jewish midnight does not correspond to 12:00 P.M. It's kind of like Jewish days starting at night and Jewish holidays coming "late" and "early." The Jewish idea of midnight requires an explanation that is beyond the scope of this glossary.)

Chol HaMoed. Passover is a weeklong festival. The first day(s) and the last day(s) have the status of being full-blown holy days, while the days in-between are a blend of both holy day and weekday. The words *Chol HaMoed* mean "the weekday portion of the festival" and refer to these intermediate days of Passover. *See* first seder.

Cleaning for Passover. On Passover, there is a prohibition against eating any leavened food products as well as a prohibition against owning and possessing such products. For this reason, people are careful to thoroughly clean their homes before Passover. This is more than just a Jewish spring-cleaning. Its central purpose is to make sure that there are no *chametz* products, or even crumbs, left anywhere in the house once Passover arrives. *See* chametz.

Cup of Elijah. In addition to the four cups of wine or grape juice that one drinks at a seder, a fifth cup is placed on the seder table. This cup is called the Cup of Elijah; it is named for Elijah the Prophet. In Jewish tradition, Elijah represents the eternal continuity of the Jewish people. It is appropriate that at the seder—where Jewish continuity is transmitted from one generation to the next—Elijah is represented. *See* four cups.

Dayenu. The word *dayenu* means "it would have been sufficient for us." This word is from one of the more famous sections in the Haggadah. The word *dayenu* is repeated throughout, and is the refrain of the song when the section is sung.

Exodus. This is the event of the Jewish people being liberated from Egyptian slavery. Led by Moses, the Jewish people walked out of Egypt and into the desert toward the promised land of Israel. The Exodus from Egypt is the pivotal moment in Jewish history. This is when the Jewish nation was born.

First days and second days. Passover begins and ends with days of *Yom Tov*, and has an in-between time known as *Chol HaMoed*. The *Yom Tov* days at the beginning of the holiday are often referred to as "the first days," while the final two *Yom Tov* days are called "the last days." *See* Yom Tov, Chol HaMoed, First seder.

First seder. This seder takes place on the first night of Passover. Not only is the Jewish calendar lunar, but in ancient times the beginning of each new lunar month was dependent on eyewitness testimony of the appearance of the moon, followed by the high court in Jerusalem—the *Sanhedrin*—officially declaring that the month had begun. When Jewish communities were established outside of Israel, they were dependent on word reaching them that the month had been declared. At times this news was delayed. Since lunar months can either be twenty-nine or thirty days, there were instances when far-flung communities weren't sure, by a day, exactly what the correct date was. To avoid the possibility of celebrating a holiday on the wrong day, the custom was adopted in the Diaspora (the Jewish communities scattered around the world) to observe both possible days. Even when there was no doubt, the custom became that Diaspora communities always observe holidays for two days while in Israel they are only observed for one. That custom remains intact to this day and therefore, in Israel, there is no first and second seder. Rather, there is just "seder night," a reference to the one-and-only-seder of Passover. Outside of Israel, where both of the first two days of Passover are holy days, there is a seder on both nights. *See* "Passover is early this year."

Four. The number four appears again and again on Passover. The most well-known instances are the four sons, four cups of wine, and four questions. The reason four is so significant at the seder is because in the Torah itself, when the story of the Exodus is told, four different adjectives are used to describe the experience of liberation.

Four cups. Within the seder are four different occasions when everyone drinks a glass of wine or grape juice.

Four questions. The seder is designed to be an interactive learning and communication experience, particularly for children. Near the beginning of the Haggadah text, four questions are posed. Each of the four questions is an elaboration on the theme, "Why is this night different from all other nights?" When there are children at the seder, it is customary to have them, particularly the youngest amongst them, ask these four questions. These questions, and the responses to them, are intended to create a general atmosphere of open questioning and discussion.

Four sons. The Haggadah text speaks about four different types of children and the different types of questions they have. By enumerating these different types of children, the Haggadah is highlighting the fact that people are different and that the means of educating and motivating them may also be different. This is a particularly important notion on an evening that is all about transmitting Jewish heritage from parent to child, from one person to the next, and from generation to generation.

Gebrukst. Some people maintain a custom that prohibits eating matzah together with a liquid. This would mean that they don't eat matzah ball soup or *matzah brei*. Why would they do something like that, you ask? The reason for this custom is as follows: If, by chance, part of a piece of matzah was not thoroughly baked, if liquid ever comes in contact with that unbaked dough, it could become *chametz*. In order to avoid any chance of eating *chametz* on Passover, some people adhere to this custom. *Gebrukst* is a Yiddish term that denotes eating matzah together with liquid.

Going away for Passover. There are two reasons why it is common for many people to spend Passover away from home.

First, since the family experience is so central to the seder, it is common for people to travel from far and wide to be together with family for Passover. Second, since Passover involves far more work and preparation than any other holiday, people are often anxious to go away for Passover and not have to deal with all the work.

Grandparents. It is common for grandparents to host the family seder when they are able, and even if they aren't hosting, it is still common to have the seder led by a grandparent. The special role of grandparents at the seder is linked to the fact that the seder is a living expression of continuity across the generations.

Grandchildren. These are the people grandparents most like to be surrounded by on Passover.

Haggadah. The Haggadah is a combination textbook, study guide, and manual for the seder. The Haggadah contains the story of the origins of the Jewish people and the events surrounding the Egyptian bondage and liberation, as well as instructions for how to fulfill all the requirements of a proper seder. Generally, the entire text of the Haggadah is read aloud at the seder.

Hand matzah. This is a traditional type of matzah where the entire production process is done by hand. The flour is mixed by hand; the dough is kneaded, rolled, and textured by hand. Then bakers place the individual unbaked matzahs into special ovens used exclusively for matzah and remove them after they are fully baked. Hand-baked matzahs are round and larger in size—as well as costlier—than machine-made matzahs.

Hiding and finding the afikomen. The *afikomen* appears twice at the seder, once early on and again near the end of the seder. Near the beginning of the seder, the person who is leading the seder wraps the *afikomen* and puts it aside for use at the end of the evening. There is a custom for the seder leader to actually hide the *afikomen* and then later dispatch the children in an effort to "find the *afikomen*." The child who finds the *afikomen* is rewarded with a special prize. This hiding and seeking of the *afikomen* is often a highlight of the seder for children of all ages.

House of Bondage. A term used to describe Egypt.

Indigestion. This frequently results from consuming one too many pieces of matzah.

Karpas. This piece of vegetable (potato, parsley, and green pepper are often used) is one of the items on the seder plate and is also used in the context of the seder. At a certain point, this vegetable is dipped into salt water—representing the tears shed by Jewish slaves—and eaten.

Kiddush. The Hebrew word *kiddush* means "distinctly spiritual." *Kiddush* is the name of the special blessing that is recited over a cup of wine on *Shabbat* and holidays. The *Kiddush* is recited at the beginning of the seder and is when everyone drinks the first of the four cups of wine.

Kosher for Passover. Foods that may be kosher at all other times are not necessarily kosher for Passover. This is because there is a unique prohibition of not eating any leavened or fermented grain products throughout the week of Passover. This means that foods like cookies, crackers, cereals, beer, breads, pastries, and the like are a no-no on Passover. The same is true of foods that contain even small amounts of grain products. So, while it's obvious that your average granola bar won't be kosher for Passover—because the main ingredients are grains—it's not self-evident that ketchup, which may also contain small amounts of ingredients derived from grain, is also off-limits for Passover. Thus, the ubiquitous "Kosher for Passover" labeling means that a particular food or food product has been produced in accordance not only with the general rules of kosher food production but also with the unique rules that apply to foods on Passover.

Leavened bread. This is conventional bread, baked after the dough has had time to rise. A Jew is not permitted to eat or even possess this kind of bread on Passover.

Machine matzah. These matzahs are made by customized baking machines that eliminate most human involvement in the baking process. You know all those boxes of matzah you see in the grocery store? They're all filled with matzahs so square only a machine could have made them.

Mah Nishtana. *Mah Nishtana* is a Hebrew phrase that

means, "Why is there a difference?" In the Hebrew text of the Haggadah, the four questions begin with this phrase. When children ask the four questions, frequently, even if the rest of the Haggadah text is read only in English, the *Mah Nishtana* is read in both Hebrew and English.

Marror. *Marror* is the bitter herb eaten at the seder as a reminder of the bitter experience of Jewish slavery. Romaine lettuce and horseradish root are commonly used as bitter herbs.

Matzah. When the Jewish people left Egypt, they didn't have time for their bread dough to rise before baking it. The result was matzah, a flat bread made from unleavened dough. Matzah is the pre-eminent symbol of Passover. The Torah proclaims that every Jew should eat matzah at least on the first night of Passover at the seder. Throughout the rest of Passover, while one does not *have* to eat matzah, it usually becomes the staple for the week because so many other kinds of foods are off limits. Matzah is great with butter or cream cheese, and can accommodate just about anything bread can. It's just that matzah leaves you with a lot more crumbs.

Matzah brei. *Matzah brei* is a holiday delicacy. *Matzah brei* is made by breaking up pieces of matzah, mixing them with eggs, and then frying them together on the stovetop. Stop by our house during Passover and I'll be happy to make you a batch.

Matzah farfel. Less fine than matzah meal, farfel is matzah broken into small pieces and is also used in many Passover recipes.

Matzah meal. This is a finely ground matzah product that is used in the cooking of many traditional Passover recipes.

"Passoveraphobia." This is a condition that afflicts people who have a fear of searching their home for crumbs, loads of extra cleaning, "bringing up dishes," and cooking for large family gatherings. The prescribed treatment is a Caribbean Passover cruise; it works every time. *See* Passover cruises, Passover hotels.

Passover cruises. Passover cruises are an example of "going away" in style. On a Passover cruise you can kill at least three birds with one stone. You don't have to do all the work of cleaning your home and preparing the meals for Passover, you have a beautiful setting for your seder (sans cooking, serving, clearing and washing dishes), and you get to enjoy a wonderful vacation, too. What could be better?

Passover dishes. The rules governing kosher for Passover food are more stringent than those governing kosher food at all other times. Because of this stringency, people who are careful to eat only kosher for Passover foods, tend to also use special dishes and utensils only for Passover. This is done to avoid the chance of any traces of non-kosher for Passover food becoming mixed with Passover food.

Passover hotels. These are hotels that transform themselves into full-service, kosher for Passover resorts for the week of the holiday. Typically, the entire dining facility is converted for Passover and a large communal seder led by a rabbi is held in the main dining room. Some families reserve smaller rooms, where they have a more intimate seder. Additionally, entertainment, educational and recreational activities are scheduled on the premises throughout the week.

"Passover is early this year." Unlike the Gregorian solar calendar that we are accustomed to, the Jewish calendar is based on the moon and not the sun. The lunar calendar and the solar calendar are not in sync, and therefore it is possible that sometimes Jewish holidays appear to be "earlier" or "later" in relation to the civil calendar.

Passover lamb. In Egypt, just prior to the tenth plague that killed all firstborn male Egyptians, God told each Jewish family to slaughter a lamb and put its blood on their doorposts. This was a sign that the home was a Jewish home and that the firstborn in that home should be spared. To the Egyptians, the lamb was a revered deity and the Jew's willingness to kill a lamb was a sign of their deep trust in God. Later, when the Temple stood in Jerusalem, there was an obligation for every family to purchase a lamb known as the "Passover offering." This lamb was brought to Jerusalem, and was eaten as part of the Passover seder. *See* afikomen.

Passover shopping. It often seems that Passover is about one thing—food, food, more food, and matzah. Because so few food products that are used during the year, other than fruits and vegetables, can be used for Passover, people need to almost completely restock their pantries and refrigerators for Passover. This need, coupled with the plethora of kosher for Passover products now available on the market, often results in a number of trips to the grocery store as people make sure that they have everything they will need for the holiday. It sometimes appears that, aside from the synagogue on the High Holidays, the largest annual community gathering of Jews takes place in the Passover section of grocery stores.

Passover wine. The drinking of four cups of wine or grape juice is a central part of the seder. Wine or grape juice used at the seder needs to be kosher for Passover. Red wine is highly preferable, but if you just can't stomach red, a Chardonnay is okay, too. I prefer a nice Merlot myself. *See* four cups.

Pesach. This is the Hebrew word for Passover. This word literally means "to skip" and is a reference to God "skipping over" the homes of the Jews during the tenth plague, the plague that killed all firstborn male Egyptians.

Pesachdik. This is actually a Yiddish word that refers to foods that are kosher for Passover or other items that are used only on Passover. *See* Passover dishes.

Pillows at the seder. In many homes, people have pillows at their seats to use when they recline. *See* reclining.

Reclining. At certain times, like when drinking the four cups, one is required to recline at the seder table. Reclining is considered a sign of royalty and independence. On the night commemorating liberation from bondage, we recline to show that we are a free people.

Roasted egg. In addition to the Passover lamb, in Temple times a second offering was brought to the Temple. This was a generic holiday offering, and it was served as the main course at the seder. The roasted egg is a reminder of that offering.

Salt water. Another symbol at the seder, the salt water represents the tears shed by Jewish slaves throughout their years of bitter slavery. *See* karpas.

Second seder. This is the seder that is celebrated on the second night of Passover everywhere other than Israel. *See* seder, first seder.

Searching for chametz. On the evening before Passover begins, a final search is made of one's home, looking for any remaining *chametz*/leavened products.

Seder. The seder is the main event of Passover and is a combination family gathering, guided study and discussion experience, and festive meal. Particular symbolic elements woven into the seder are meant to recall the experience of the Exodus and the birth of the Jewish people. A text, the Haggadah, is read and discussed at the seder. The Haggadah text tells the story of the Exodus, and touches on a variety of themes central to Passover. The Passover seder is understood to be a primary venue for the transmission of Jewish identity and commitment from one generation to the next.

Seder guests. The seder is a celebration of Jewish peoplehood and is not meant to be a solitary experience. First and foremost, the seder is a family experience; however, beyond immediate family, it is an experience meant to involve the larger family of the Jewish people. It is very common for people hosting a seder to go out of their way to invite guests in addition to their own family. Many families actively seek out people who may not have a place for a seder and invite them to join their seder.

Seder plate. Much of the seder revolves around a group of symbolic items including a roasted egg, a vegetable, bitter herbs and others. The seder plate is a specially designed, ornamental dish upon which these objects are arranged. The seder plate is set in front of the person leading the seder, and its contents are periodically referred to throughout the seder.

Selling chametz. Since the owning of *chametz* is prohibited on Passover, one is obligated to discard *chametz* prior to the onset of the holiday. In cases where one owns large quantities of *chametz*, it can be sold to a non-Jew and then repurchased after Passover ends. This is a specialized sale that is generally conducted through a rabbi who draws up a contract that reflects Jewish law. This sale is not merely for appearance's sake, and is not considered a valid sale unless the buyer has the full right to retain ownership if he chooses.

Shank bone. This small piece of roasted meat on the seder plate is a reminder of the Passover lamb that was a part of the seder in the era when the Jewish people lived in Israel and the Temple stood in Jerusalem.

Shmura matzah. The word *shmura* means "guarded." This guarding refers to the flour used to bake matzah. Guarded *shmura* flour is supervised from the time the wheat is harvested all the way through the baking process. The purpose of this supervision is to ensure that no liquid comes in contact with the flour. This is important because moisture can begin a premature leavening process that could result in non-kosher matzah. The guarding of most matzah flour begins with the manufacturing process and not as early as the time of harvesting. *Shmura* flour and *shmura* matzah is a kind of "extra credit" stringency that is not absolutely required.

"Turning over the kitchen." A wonderful transformation takes place when an ordinary kitchen is transformed into a Passover kitchen. The annual ritual of replacing the regular kitchenwares—dishes, cutlery, and other items—with Passover wares is known as "turning over the kitchen."

Unleavened bread. This is another term for matzah.

"Where will you be for the seder?" Because it is so common for families to travel to be together for the Passover seder, people regularly ask one another questions like, "Are you going away for Passover?" or "Where will you be for the seder?"

Yom Tov. *Yom Tov* is a generic term that is usually translated as holiday. In actuality, the term *Yom Tov* denotes those particularly holy days on which certain specific rules of Jewish law apply. In that sense, *Yom Tov* days are similar to *Shabbat* (the Sabbath), which also has a whole set of unique and specific rules, though the two differ in a number of ways. One major distinction is that cooking is forbidden on *Shabbat*, while it is permitted on *Yom Tov*. Passover is a weeklong holiday. The first two days and the last two days of Passover are days of *Yom Tov*, while the intermediate days are just quasi-*Yom Tov*. *See* Chol HaMoed.

let's do

Passover!

3

A Step-by-Step Guide to the
Essentials of Celebrating Passover

No question about it, when it comes to Passover, there's a lot
to do. There is certainly more to do before Passover than there is
before any other holiday, and even when Passover begins, there
is also more to do than during any other holiday. This chapter
will focus on the main events that precede Passover—namely,
preparing one's home and getting rid of any *chametz*—and the
big show itself, the Passover seder.

Cleaning for Passover

What: The purpose of cleaning your home prior to Passover
is to make sure that when the holiday begins, there is no *chametz*
left in your home, as well as to ensure that no *chametz* becomes
mixed into any foods that are prepared for eating on Passover.
Passover cleaning does *not* mean that every single item in your
home has to be cleaned and polished; rather, it means that your
home has to be "clean" of any *chametz*.

How: For the sake of Passover cleaning, the home can be divided into two general areas: places where food is regularly stored and eaten, and places where food is generally not taken. I will give some examples of each and a brief description of how Passover cleaning works for each.

Kitchen/dining room: All *chametz* food items (*see* p. 20) must either be eaten, disposed of, or sold. Floors, countertops, and tables, where one would expect to find crumbs, should be carefully cleaned. Dishes, cutlery, and other items used in food preparation throughout the year are not used during Passover.

Ovens/stovetops: Ovens need to be thoroughly cleaned and run through the self-cleaning cycle before cooking Passover foods in them. Stovetops should be thoroughly cleaned, and then the burners should be turned to the highest position, and left there for a few minutes before using them to cook for Passover.

Bedrooms: Unless your spouse regularly brings you breakfast in bed, all you need to do is give your bedroom a good sweeping. If you have children who may sneak a candy bar, pretzels or a sandwich into their rooms, then you—or better yet, they—need to check the room more carefully. You never know when an old pizza crust is going to show up under a child's bed.

Bathrooms, basements and so on: These areas should be cleaned as they normally would be.

When: Too often, I approach life with the following attitude: "Why procrastinate when I can just push things off for a few days?" When it comes to Passover cleaning, I highly recommend a different approach. Don't wait until the last minute! Give yourself enough time to do a thorough job of making sure that, once Passover arrives, your home will be *chametz*-free.

Why: The prototypical form of *chametz* is bread. Matzah, the alter ego of bread, is simply dough that was never allowed to ferment and rise. The most obvious difference between bread and matzah—one is flat, while the other is all puffed up—is also the most significant.

As a rule, Judaism encourages creativity, initiative, and striving for personal growth and meaningful accomplishments. At the same time, the Torah is mindful of our susceptibility to being carried away by pride in our achievements, and conscious of the havoc that can be wreaked by an over-inflated ego. Few things are more destructive than an ego run amok. On Passover, puffy, leavened bread comes to represent the big-headed swagger of arrogance. As we rid our exterior domain, the homes we live in, of *chametz*, we simultaneously strive to liberate our inner domain, our consciousness of self, from the grips of an over-inflated ego. This experience of attempting to view ourselves, and to live, free of the excesses of ego—at least for a week—enables us to reestablish a balanced picture of who we are, who we aren't, and who we truly want to be.

Searching for *chametz*

What: On the night before the first seder, there is a formal obligation to make a careful and final check of one's home for *chametz*. This is known as *bedikat chametz*, the checking for *chametz*.

How: This room-by-room search is done by the light of a candle or flashlight. Before beginning the search, a blessing is recited, and then the search begins. In each room of the house, you dim the lights, and then, using your candle or flashlight (a much safer choice), you look in the corners, the hard-to-reach places, and all the nooks and crannies for any remnants of *chametz*. Any *chametz* that is found is carefully put aside to be burnt the next morning. When you have finished searching the entire house, a special declaration is recited stating that you relinquish ownership of any *chametz* that may inadvertently be left in your home.

When: The time for conducting this search is after nightfall on the evening before the first seder. If you will be away from home that night, then the search can be performed on an earlier night.

Why: *Chametz* is Passover's great antagonist. Passover is the holiday of liberation, matzah is that unique kind of bread that represents liberation, and on a spiritual plane the essence of the holiday is the achievement of an inner liberation—a freedom of the spirit. *Chametz*, on the other hand, represents everything that stands between us and the achievement of freedom. On the eve of Passover, as we search our homes for *chametz*, we are also supposed to be looking inward for all issues that stand between us and freedom.

Blessing

This blessing is said just prior to beginning the search for *chametz*:

בָּרוּךְ אַתָּה ה׳ אֱלֹהֵינוּ מֶלֶךְ הָעוֹלָם
אֲשֶׁר קִדְּשָׁנוּ בְּמִצְוֹתָיו וְצִוָּנוּ עַל בִּיעוּר חָמֵץ.

*"Baruch atah Adonai, Eloheynu melech ha-olam,
asher kidshanu b'mitzvotav, v'tzivanu al bi'ur chametz."*

"Blessed are You, Adonai our God, King of the Universe,
Who has made us holy through His commandments and has
commanded us regarding the removal of *chametz*."

Declaration

This declaration is said when the search for *chametz* is completed:

כָּל חֲמִירָא וַחֲמִיעָא דְּאִיכָּא בִרְשׁוּתִי דְּלָא חֲמִתֵּיהּ וּדְלָא בְעַרְתֵּיהּ
וּדְלָא יְדַעְנָא לֵיהּ לִבְטַל וְלֶהֱוֵי הֶפְקֵר בְּעַפְרָא דְאַרְעָא.

*"Kol chamira v'chamiyah d'iykah birshutee,
d'loh chamitay u'd'loh bi'artai u'd'loh ya'danah lay,
livtail, u'l'hevai hefker k'afrah d'arah."*

"All leaven and leaven bread in my possession, that which I
have not seen or removed, or am unaware of, should be annulled
and considered ownerless, like the dust of the earth."

Burning *chametz*

What: In addition to cleaning and searching for *chametz*, there is an obligation to actually destroy any remaining remnants of *chametz*.

How: The traditional way that this destruction is done is by making a small fire and burning whatever *chametz* was found during the final search. Practically speaking, since homes are frequently *chametz*-free even before the final search begins, what many people do is put aside some bread or other *chametz* specifically for this burning. If burning is impractical, your remaining *chametz* can be thrown into a pond or stream or can even be flushed down the toilet.

When: This burning is done during the morning preceding the first seder. Following the burning of the *chametz*, the declaration that was read the night before is read again.

Why: Our sages have a saying: "When you have an opportunity to do a *mitzvah* (a Divine directive), don't let it spoil in your hand." In other words, watch out for procrastination, because the result is often a golden opportunity gone sour. The Hebrew word for "spoil" is *chametz*. Wine that has turned to vinegar is called *chametz*. Let's be honest, most of us have an inclination to procrastinate, and probably all of us have paid dearly for it. When we burn our *chametz*, deep inside we are also attempting to burn away the urge to procrastinate—at least for a week.

The Seder

What: The seder is an experiential, educational family dinner designed to communicate and transmit the story of the Exodus and its timeless lessons from one generation of Jews to the next.

How: The "how" of the seder is so involved that there is actually a how-to manual for the seder. It's called the Haggadah. The Haggadah contains all of the instructions and information necessary to conduct a seder. The real answer to "How does one conduct a seder?" is that you need to sit down and read through an entire Haggadah. (If you were to ask my mother, she would recommend you read *The Survival Kit Family Haggadah*.)

In a nutshell, a seder has two primary aspects. There is the reading and discussing of the text contained in the Haggadah, and then there is the carrying out of the various observances that are unique to the seder. These observances include eating matzah, drinking four cups of wine, eating bitter herbs, dipping a piece of vegetable in saltwater, and a whole lot more.

When: The seder is celebrated on each of the first two nights of Passover (or in Israel, just on the first night).

Why: The Hebrew word seder means "order" or "sequence," and it is the Haggadah that is the guide to the entire sequence of events that takes place at the seder. The word *Haggadah* means to "tell" or to "relate." The Haggadah is a vivid, step-by-step narrative set in the context of a parent-child dialogue. The seder, with the Haggadah as its focus, tells every Jew three things: who you are, where you came from, and what you stand for. The message inherent in the Haggadah is that Jewish identity and continuity hinge on encouraging children to ask questions, and being prepared as parents to provide sensitive and substantive answers.

Without a doubt, the seder is the main event of Passover, and the Haggadah is absolutely essential to the seder. For this reason, the next two chapters will deal exclusively with the seder and the Haggadah.

the Passover
Puzzle

4

Of Seders and Shortcuts

The Hebrew word *seder* means "order," and relates to the fact that the seder follows a precise order, embodied in the fifteen sequential experiences that comprise the seder. *Seder* implies a necessary sequence of events. This means that, while shortcuts may be convenient, they can also be illusory. Sure, you can figure out an ingenious route to sneak around rush hour traffic or curl up with a single volume containing ten-page summaries of everything from Shakespeare to Stephen King, but, in matters that truly count, shortcuts may not be the best idea. They don't work when it comes to raising children or building a marriage, and certainly not with personal and spiritual growth. Deeper living just doesn't flourish in the land of quick fixes. As a rule, only seder, only order, will do.

Over the centuries, many great scholars have revealed a wealth of ideas about the deeper meanings of the fifteen orderly aspects of the seder and how they are interrelated. We will touch upon some of these ideas in the coming pages.

FIFTEEN PIECES OF THE PASSOVER PUZZLE

1. KADESH
A special blessing is recited over a glass of wine. This blessing speaks of the treasured role that all holidays play in Jewish life and makes particular reference to Passover.

2. URECHATZ
Prior to eating the *karpas* (vegetable), everyone at the seder washes his or her hands in the prescribed manner.

3. KARPAS
A small piece of vegetable is dipped in saltwater and eaten.

4. YACHATZ
The person leading the seder takes the middle matzah and breaks it in half. The larger half becomes the *afikomen* and the smaller half is returned to its place.

5. MAGGID
This is the reading and discussion of the Haggadah text. At least half of the seder is devoted to discussing the Exodus from Egypt.

6. RACHTZAH
After completing the Haggadah, people wash their hands before eating the matzah and beginning the meal. A blessing is recited by each individual after the washing.

7. MOTZI
The blessing recited before eating the first piece of matzah.

8. MATZAH
Everyone eats a piece of matzah.

9. MAROR
A blessing is recited and the bitter herbs are eaten.

10. KORECH
Having just eaten matzah and bitter herbs separately, they are now eaten together as a sandwich.

11. SHULCHAN ORECH
Finally! The festive Passover meal is enjoyed by all.

12. TZAFUN
The *afikomen*, which had been hidden earlier, is now brought back and everyone eats a piece of matzah as a personal *afikomen*.

13. BARECH
These blessings are said at the conclusion of every meal. At the seder, they contain special references to Passover.

14. HALLEL
The songs of praise authored by King David are recited.

15. NIRTZAH
A short prayer is recited expressing the hope that we successfully fulfilled all the observances of the seder. The prayer captures our hopes for a brighter future in the words, "Next year in Jerusalem."

The Passover Puzzle

The holiday of Passover is known as *z'man cheruteynu*—the season of our freedom. The seder is the centerpiece of this "season of freedom" and, like the emergent picture formed by the pieces of some fantastic jigsaw puzzle, is designed to create a vivid experiential image of what freedom is all about. But these are no ordinary puzzle pieces, and this is no ordinary puzzle. This is a puzzle made of metaphysical pieces that are affected by the way the person holding them relates to them. It is through the careful and thoughtful handling of each piece that its inherent form begins to emerge. Further, it is our thoughts and understanding of the intrinsic nature of these rebus-like pieces that actually reveal their true color, imagery, and light. Once assembled, they create a brilliant mosaic of freedom, the freedom of a Jewish soul. A soul that soars on its own powerful wings, and that is part of the great majestic soul of the Jewish people. A soul guided by wisdom, and inspired by everything the Jewish people has ever stood for. This vibrant totality becomes visible through the piece-by-piece assembly of the seder experience, and in turn works its way into the very fabric of our being.

The ideas that follow give merely a glimpse into the world of insight contained in each of the fifteen pieces of the Passover puzzle. It is my hope that the ideas related here will serve as a relevant starting point as you approach your experience at the seder, your assembly of these marvelous pieces of wisdom, and your Passover odyssey of freedom.

1. *Kadesh*—
The recitation of the *kiddush* blessing
over a glass of wine or grape juice.

The seder is a world within a world. The words *kadesh* and *kiddush* are derived from the word *kadosh*. Though commonly translated as "holy" or "sanctified," *kadosh* actually means "separate" or "distinct."

The first piece in our puzzle—*kadesh*—summons us to step into the distinctive world of Passover. A world filled with feelings, *mitzvot* (commandments), customs and ideas, all of which point the way to freedom. This very act of separation begins to move us toward a deeper awareness of ourselves and what it will take to achieve the prized freedom of Passover.

Sometimes, "just getting away from things" is precisely what is needed to gain a fresh perspective on the situation of our lives. By separating ourselves from routine, we are able to reflect on where we are, how we got there, what's driving us, and what our goals are. Then, with a bit more clarity, we can address the question, "Where do we go from here?"

On the seder night, we "get away" to a place filled with Jewish ideas about freedom and about life. From within the sacred realm of the seder, we look back and imagine a life empowered by our noblest inclinations and vivified by a commitment to making the world the kind of place Judaism believes it can be.

2. Urechatz—
Washing the hands before eating the *karpas*.

If you ask someone what comes first, the house or the blueprints, the answer you are most likely to receive is, "the blueprints, of course." The truth, however, is quite the opposite. Before you can create a set of prints, you first need a vision of the home you want to build. In a prayer that is part of the Friday evening *Shabbat* service, we find the words *soaf ma-aseh bemachshava techillah*, which means "every goal must precede itself in thought." First comes a completed house in conceptual form—the goal—and only then are blueprints drawn up and a house finally built.

Throughout the year, it is the practice to wash one's hands only before eating bread or matzah, but two millennia ago, when the Temple stood in Jerusalem, Jews also washed before eating other types of foods. The washing before the *karpas* is reminiscent of life in an altogether different time and place. After having entered the dimension of Passover by way of the *kiddush*, *urechatz* now tells us to stop and focus on another era—on the ancient city of Jerusalem—and on other goals—on the timeless ideas that are at the heart of Jerusalem.

Freedom means being a virtuoso of the spirit. It's having a panoramic awareness of the full range of one's drives, dreams, impulses and abilities—and being their master. Freedom means more than the license to gratify impulses on demand. Only with freedom can the full force of one's being be brought to bear on the realization of life's ultimate goals. All of this is inherent in the meaning of Jerusalem. More than just the seat of ancient Jewish sovereignty, the restored Jerusalem that Jews have always dreamt of is one from which all mankind will draw spiritual inspiration and insight. Jerusalem is the embodiment of our goals and our mission. Born in the darkness of Egypt, we have been called to be "a light unto the nations." Our destiny is to be a spiritual conduit—with Jerusalem as the nexus—through which enlightenment will come to the world.

Jerusalem, with the Temple at its heart, is where we develop our most intimate relationship with a sublime Creator. From there we are stirred to translate the energy of that relationship into a passionate pursuit of our destiny as a people. The dream of Jerusalem—the dream of humankind achieving a state where it is both human and kind—is the dream of every Jewish soul.

Right from the start, *urechatz* tells us to lift our eyes and gaze at a vision of our deepest dreams, because every goal must precede itself in thought. *Urechatz* is another piece in the puzzle, and another move toward freedom.

3. Karpas—
Dipping a piece of vegetable in saltwater and eating it.

Karpas draws our thoughts to true human beauty, and to truly beautiful human beings. Try this—

✦ Close your eyes and picture someone who you consider to be a beautiful human being, someone who embodies the finest qualities a person can possess.

✦ Now ask yourself if it isn't that person's capacity to be a giver that allows you to identify him or her as beautiful. Isn't it a penchant for being outwardly-focused and other-centered that you find to be so beautiful? Isn't it the person's benevolence, compassion and sincere concern for the well-being of others?

We are transfixed by an artist's talent and a musician's melody. We are envious of the Fortune 500 CEO. Yet the quality of beauty is not one we necessarily attach to any of these men or women of achievement. Intuitively, however, we associate giving with beauty, and thus, almost instinctively, we try to raise children who are "givers" and not "takers." A doctor, a professor, an athlete, or even an author—but never at the expense of being a self-centered taker. To be beautiful is to be a giver.

Listen to *karpas*, in Hebrew.

Hebrew: The Fantasia of Language

In the Hebrew language, every letter is not only a letter but also a number, a word and a concept. As an example, the letter *aleph*, the first letter of the alphabet, has the numerical value of one. *Aleph* is also a word that means "to champion" or "to lead." The second letter of the alphabet, *beit*, has the numerical value of two and also means "house." Hebrew letters, then, are far more than mere letters but are actually linguistic repositories for concepts and ideas. It follows that Hebrew words, too, are not an amalgam of random sounds, but precise constructs of the conceptual components that form them.

When we analyze the word *karpas* and break it down to its four component parts, its four letters, what we discover is an embedded message that teaches a basic lesson about how to polish our capacity for giving.

The Hebrew word *karpas* is constructed of four letters: *kaf, reish, peh*, and *samech*. These four letters are also four words, and when taken together they steer our mind's eye toward an essential aspect of giving.

כ	Kaf	Palm of the hand
ר	Reish	A poor person
פ	Peh	Mouth
ס	Samech	To support

The word *kaf*, the first letter in *karpas*, means "palm of the hand." The palm is exposed when the hand is open—in a giving mode. The word *reish* means "a poor person." When taken together, these first two letter-words represent a hand that is opened to someone in need. Thus we have the classic image of giving, one who has more, lending assistance to one who has less. But what if you are a person of limited means? What if you simply have little to give? The second half of the word *karpas* reminds us that there are many roads to becoming a giver. The letter *peh* means "mouth," while the final letter, *samech*, means "to support." True, you may not be capable of giving in the material sense, but you can always give with your words—words of kindness and concern, words of empathy and understanding, words that can lift an impoverished soul and provide a means of support where nothing else will do.

✦ ✦ ✦ ✦ ✦

The karpas is dipped in saltwater before it is eaten. The saltwater is meant to recall the bitter tears shed in Egypt. But there is more. The Jewish people, though awash in the tears of bondage, were able to preserve their ability to give. Rather then succumb to the morass of self-pity, they were able to maintain their dignity by maintaining their beauty—the beauty born of giving.

4. *Yachatz*—
The middle piece of matzah is broken in half.
The smaller piece is returned to its place, while the larger one is wrapped and put aside to serve later as the *afikomen*.

If a friend needed to borrow one of our cars for a couple of days, I'm sure my wife and I would try to be accommodating. On the other hand, if they needed it for a month or two, we would have to apologize and explain that we really can't manage with just one car.
Recently, something happened that forced us to rethink

this position. One of our cars broke down. And it took a month to get the right parts! So how did we deal with this suburban catastrophe? Did we rent? Did we borrow? Did we steal? No, we simply managed. With an adjustment here, some juggling over there, and an added bit of patience all around, we were able to adjust our schedules, give one another rides, make alternative arrangements, and barely miss a beat in our busy schedules. We also had the pleasure of some extra time together.

Funny, isn't it? There are so many possessions that we simply "can't live without," until of course we have to. But mind you, our new bread maker is a different story altogether. We really can't live without that!

So you want to be a giver, only you think you have nothing to give. Not in the material sense and not even in the emotional or spiritual sense. Well, think again. Quite often our inability to give and to share is the product of a skewed picture of reality. Many of our limitations are only perceived limitations, fictitious barriers that many before us have overcome and others just like us will continue to surmount.

This is *yachatz*. The middle matzah is broken in two, the larger piece is hidden away, and the smaller piece returns to its place and continues to fulfill its function despite the loss. No, this is not a suggestion that you go out and intentionally smash your second (or third) car, trade in your microwave for a Bunsen burner, or cut your sleeping hours in half, but it is a suggestion to pause and think twice.

If your brother or sister needed some of your time, money, or a piece of your heart, would you not find a way to give it to him or her? Humankind is one big extended family, and Jews are all brothers and sisters. Just as there are plenty of needs, there are also plenty of resources, if only we realize how much we have available to give, and how much we truly want to give.

5. *Maggid—*
Reading the main body of the Haggadah text.

Would it really be such a big deal if parents never taught their children to say "thank you"? Obviously it would be, because if you don't say thank you, you're an ingrate. And just like no one wants to be an ingrate, no one wants to marry one, be friends with one, or raise one. That's why parents teach the "magic words."

Ingrates tend to end up in a prison of their own design. Their ego-obsessed lack of gratitude erects impenetrable walls that lock the world out and shut the ingrate in.

The Talmud teaches that the thematic flow of the Haggadah narrative is meant to sensitize us to one of life's most basic traits of self-liberation—gratitude. The textual flow of the Haggadah follows a pattern known as "opening with the ignominious and concluding with the praiseworthy." It is for this reason that the Haggadah begins by highlighting the less-than-flattering origins of the Jewish people—"we were slaves to Pharaoh in Egypt... Our forefathers were idol worshippers..."—and concludes with our triumphant liberation and the formation of a unique relationship with God. This recurrent theme of contrasting lowly origins with ennobled achievements is meant to sensitize us to the trait that stands as the ingrate's staunchest rival—gratitude.

Those successful men and women who forget their humble origins and eschew the commoners who helped them achieve their success are doomed to occupy a cell, plush though it may be, inhabited only by themselves and a gaggle of smiling opportunists-cum-friends. As ingratitude builds walls, two truly magical words, "thank you," are able to build bridges—from person to person, and from people to God.

Todah: Another Look at Thank You
The Hebrew word for "thank you" is *todah*, which literally means "to admit." When we say thank you, we are making an admission. We are admitting that we needed someone else. You passed me the salt, helped me in business, changed my tire, or

raised me as a child. To say thank you means to admit that "I couldn't have done it without you." Beneath it all, when we express our gratitude, be it to a person or to God, we are recognizing our dependence on another and acknowledging the kind assistance we received. And, though dependence is never easy to admit, when graciously acknowledged, it facilitates harmony, bonding and freedom.

6. Rachtzah—
Washing the hands prior to eating the matzah

Sometimes it feels like we are prisoners of our past, but it doesn't have to be that way. *Rachtzah* is about our ability to make changes in life. Probably nothing is more liberating than knowing that just because things have always been a certain way, that doesn't mean they always have to be that way. Judaism insists that we possess the ability to cleanse ourselves of corrosive habits that stymie our efforts for fulfilled living. If life is about growth and growth means change, then freedom is not, as Janis Joplin said, "just another word for nothing left to lose," but rather, "Freedom's just another word..." for change! Or, as William James put it, "The greatest discovery of my generation is that a human being can alter his life by altering his attitude."

Rachtzah is exactly what it appears to be. It is a washing away of those rusty attitudinal routines that threaten to lock our lives into a holding pattern of mediocrity. The most liberating thought is the recognition of the possibility of liberation. To realize that one is capable of change qualitatively alters the rules of the game. Where once the deck seemed to be stacked against you, the odds are now clearly in your favor.

7. Motzi—
The blessing recited before eating the first piece of matzah

The blessing we say for matzah is the same blessing we say before eating bread. "Blessed are you, Hashem, our God, King of the universe—*hamotzi lechem min ha-aretz*—who brings forth bread from the ground."

If you think about it, this blessing doesn't seem to be giving credit where credit is due. Granted, God may bring forth wheat from the ground, but when was the last time you saw a farmer harvesting loaves of bread? Bread comes from the ovens of bakers and grandmothers, not "from the ground." And if you want to be a stickler about this, you could argue that God doesn't even deserve all the credit for the wheat. Isn't the farmer the one who prepares the soil for planting, properly sows the seeds, and then harvests the crop at just the right time? If anything, the production of bread and matzah is a partnership, with God acting as the junior partner.

An idea in *halacha* (Jewish law) seems to reinforce the problem with the way the blessing of *hamotzi* is worded. The *halacha* states that upon saying *hamotzi* one should be careful to hold the loaf with all ten fingers. This is to remind us that the production of bread is a ten-step process. From the preparation of the soil to the planting, harvesting, grinding, and right through the kneading and baking of the dough is a full ten steps. Aren't all of these steps in the hands of man, as the *halacha* implies, and not in the hands of God, as the blessing implies?

The Partnership of Man and God

Consider this: When I floss my teeth and forestall the creeping advances of tooth and gum decay, do I deserve a pat on the back and a round of applause? Do I hold my head high and flash a proud, contented smile? Or, do I say, "Thank God I've got the brains and ability to prevent my teeth from becoming premature mush"?

Judaism says, take pleasure—not pride—in the constructive choices you make in life. The Jewish view of the man-God partnership boils down to this: You make the sensible choice to floss your teeth. The rest is a gift—the cognitive aptitude necessary to grasp the hygienist's instructions on how to floss, the ability to consistently judge whether or not you've pulled out the right amount of floss, the dexterity required to gently maneuver the floss between your tooth and gums. Each of these disparate abilities, along with countless others, are gifts from God. Our job is to partner with God.

A fresh loaf of bread, like a well-flossed tooth, is a marvelous accomplishment. We take pleasure in our accomplishments and are thankful that we chose to use our many gifts in a constructive and meaningful manner.

8. *Matzah*—
Eating the first piece of matzah

9. *Maror*—
Eating the bitter herbs

10. *Korech*—
Eating the sandwich of matzah and maror

11. *Shulchan Orech*—
Eating the festive meal.

12. *Tzafun*—
Eating the afikomen, the hidden piece of matzah

These five pieces of the Passover puzzle are each centered on eating, and together they form one supra-piece. When taken together, these pieces provide a sweeping view of the essential spiritual make-up of every human being. In doing so, they simultaneously reveal a path for successfully engaging the ever-present physicality of our existence.

The Continuum of Human Spirituality

Human beings, ladybugs, angels and dolphins all have one thing in common—each is a being created by God. Imagine a spectrum of created beings. At one end of the spectrum are purely spiritual entities, like angels, while the other end is populated by purely physical beings, like cows. The question is this: Where on this continuum do people fit in? "Well," you might think to yourself, "some people I know come close to the spiritual end, while others seem to belong to the end where grazing is the dominant activity of the day."

The Jewish concept is that human beings, unique creatures that we are, are a blend of both ends of the spectrum. That is, each and every one of us is part angel and part cow, part spiritual and part physical.*

Take a look for yourself. Isn't there something within you—an angelic core—that is inclined toward the spiritual, toward that which transcends the mundanity of the corporeal world? Isn't there a dimension of your being that yearns to dispense with its preoccupation with food, sleep and comfort? That longs to be free to pursue the eternal and not the transitory, to experience that which is intensely meaningful and not fleeting or petty?

Now look again. Isn't there also a part of you that longs to spend endless sun-massaged days on a quiet beach with chilled beverages at your side, CDs playing your favorite music, and the Sunday paper, while drifting away from all your cares, worries and responsibilities?

That's just the way we are. A not-always-harmonious blend of spiritual and physical. One moment we are selflessly seeking to better the lot of all mankind and the next we are in a huff over the delivery of a pizza without the extra cheese. One morning we are inspired to find private time to meditate and reflect or to nurture our spousal intimacy, and then by lunchtime we are back in full-throttled pursuit of wealth, success and acclaim. This is all of us. It is the conundrum of our existence, and the dynamic to which the matzah and *maror* allude.

Matzah is the soul. When pared of his or her external trappings and physical interests, you will find that something yet remains of the human being—the longing of the soul, the essential nucleus of self. Likewise a loaf of bread, when stripped of all its additives—of sugar and salt, of poppy seeds or raisins, and even of time to rise—an essence still remains. Stripped-down bread is matzah, and a stripped-down human being is a soul.

For an entire week we eat only matzah and consider only our deepest aspirations and loftiest dreams. Like an unwieldy corporate monster that has become diversified beyond recognition, with matzah we now try to get back to the basics—

---

*For a more in-depth treatment of the spiritual nature of human beings, see *Judaism in a Nutshell: God* (Leviathan Press, 2001).

to focus not only on priorities but also on the basic values and goals that define our priorities. Ultimately, to reconnect with that inner force that once promised to animate our every move.

Maror, on the other hand, is our physicality run amok. To demean the body and shun the world of physical pleasures is never the way of Judaism. Rather, Judaism asserts what all of us know. If you eat too much ice cream, you get sick; if you eat ice cream too fast, you won't taste it; and if you eat ice cream too often, eventually you will lose your taste for ice cream.

The alternative, the Jewish path to both ice cream and spirituality, is to master our desires for the delicious. The bitter herbs are not a call to ascetic denial but rather a reminder of one of life's earliest learned truths, that for a cow a life guided by moment-to-moment physical needs and urges is fine, perhaps even sweet, but for us—angels that we are—that lifestyle can get a little bitter. Remember this lesson and you are halfway to becoming an authentic connoisseur—of life.

Korech is the most precise picture of who we are. We are neither the unencumbered soul of the Brahman nor the untamed body of a gluttonous boor. Rather, as two hydrogen atoms adhere to one of oxygen and form a new entity called water, so a soul when fused with a body becomes the crowning element of creation—a striving, struggling, growing, free-willed, creative human being. Those who master the tensions of this duality, who can achieve a spiritually driven balance, who are able to live like a soul while dressing like a body, are ready to move on to *Shulchan Orech*.

Shulchan Orech offers a grand view of life that sees the world as an exquisitely set table of delicious opportunities for growth, a banquet without end. Know your essence, beware the bitter herbs, and harmonize the totality of your being in the service of your greatest goals. Then—and only then—will the delicacies of living truly be open before you.

Tzafun means concealment and depicts ultimate potential. We bring the *afikomen* out of its place of hiding and with it we bring a message of the hidden potential in every aspect of creation.

The *afikomen* represents the Passover lamb (*see* page 27) that was eaten by every Jew when the Temple stood in Jerusalem. The *halacha* (Jewish law) regarding the Passover lamb states:

(1) that it must be eaten only after the Passover meal has been concluded; and

(2) that nothing may be eaten after the lamb. In effect, it is lamb chops and not macaroons that are the Passover dessert of tradition. Today, the same rules apply to the *afikomen*. It is only eaten at the end of the meal, and it is to be the last food we taste at the seder. The *afikomen* is not consumed because we are hungry but only because it is a *mitzvah*, a spiritual directive.

Generally, when we eat, it is to satisfy our appetite—but not at the seder. On the night of the seder, the *afikomen* points to eating not as an end but as an enabler, to physical pleasures as an aid and not as an aim.

Ultimately, the intended state of the physical world is that of a vast toolshed overflowing with devices designed to help us access a higher reality. When properly understood, the hidden potential of our physicality is to connect us to a spiritual dimension stored in every corner of creation.

This is the secret of eating the hidden piece of matzah. Every aspect of life—every person and every fruit, every moment and every blade of grass—possesses ultimate potential. Like the latent forces of energy stored up in the atom, the potential of spirituality is waiting inside every morsel of life. And once you experience this, once you taste the subtle flavors of *afikomen*, you won't want to taste anything else.

13. *Barech*—
Birkat Hamazon, the blessing recited at the end of the meal

Life is a struggle, a challenge, and frequently quite difficult. Above all, though, life is a blessing. The Hebrew word for blessing, *bracha*, is closely related to the word *breicha*, which means a free-flowing spring of water. Once we have grappled with our goals, striven to clarify our spiritual ambitions, and fought tooth and nail to master the conflict of body and soul, then we can view life with all the freshness of a clear, living stream.

A comfortably middle-aged couple from suburbia was visiting Israel for the first time. In Israel, all roads lead to Jerusalem. It was there that they struck up a conversation with an American who had recently settled in Jerusalem. They stood beneath the Western Wall and they talked. In the shadow of Jewish history yet unfolding, thoughts and feelings co-mingled as one.

"What made you move to Israel?" they asked.

"Israel," they were assured, "is a freshly prepared canvas; here you can touch your brush to the palette of life and use the colors of your soul and your history to paint your future and destiny."

This is the feeling of blessing—a canvas full of life and hope and promise just waiting to be painted. A sense of overwhelming potential and vibrant optimism, firmly rooted in reality while freely reaching for the stars.

14. *Hallel*—
The songs of praise

My grandfather once helped a young man break through what was then an almost impenetrable racial barrier, and that man went on to become one of the most respected members of Congress. My grandfather gave him a job, an opportunity and hope, where society said he must not. My grandfather was tough, encouraging, and a friend. My grandfather is not with us anymore, but whenever given the opportunity, one man who had a long and honored career on Capitol Hill continues to sing his praises.

A Jewish cadet at West Point was taking a course on modern warfare—Korea, Vietnam, Afghanistan, Iran-Iraq, the Falklands, and even the invasion of Grenada. Each was carefully analyzed for lessons that might be applied to future conflicts involving U.S. troops.

Well into the curriculum, this cadet had a question. Why was it, he asked a commander, that not one battle involving Israel was ever studied? Not the Israeli War of Independence, fought by a tankless, planeless "army" of hastily trained soldiers and Holocaust survivors against a well-armed invasion force; not the Six Day War, which Arab leaders promised would be the Jews' final dying breath; not the Yom Kippur War, which snatched near disaster from the jaws of one of histories largest sneak attacks; not a single one.

Could these glaring omissions be reflective of an anti-Semitic blind spot? Could Americans not stoop to learn how to fight from Jews? No, the cadet was assured, this was no ethnically derisive oversight. Those wars just weren't normal. The things that took place in all the battles that birthed and defended the Jews of Israel just don't happen anywhere else. It doesn't pay to study them, the cadet was informed, because there is nothing for other countries to learn.

From the liberation in Egypt to the impossible rebirth of Israel, it sometimes seems that little has changed. At the seder, we feel the freedom of our history. We're free of the historical strings that seem to bind people to the predictable routes of nations and civilizations, free of every societal force that attempts to restrict us to its path, its ideals.

At the seder, we are free to be Jews—to be the Jewish people—to make a difference. And we are free to sing the praises of the One who broke the chains of bondage and set us free.

15. *Nirtzah*—
Next year in Jerusalem—*L'shana haba b'Yerushalayim*

Every synagogue in the world faces Jerusalem. In prayer—whether in a synagogue, at home, or in an open meadow—every Jewish heart is directed toward Jerusalem. As the *ne'ilah* service draws to a close at the conclusion of Yom Kippur, congregations the world over proclaim, "Next year in Jerusalem." Every groom breaks a glass under the *chuppah* and for a moment all thoughts are on Jerusalem. And again on Passover, in the waning moments of the seder, every Jewish family prays—Next year in Jerusalem, *L'shana haba b'Yerushalayim.*

The name Jerusalem means "city of peace." Peace, *shalom*, is not merely the absence of conflict. Neither is it a utilitarian notion of cooperation and coexistence. Peace is the seamless harmony of individuals genuinely embracing a common vision. Not that each becomes lost in some faceless wave of the masses but that each aspires to lend the beauty of his or her potential to the realization of a transcendent mission.

With *nirtzah*, with our eyes on the city of peace, we have come full circle. The pieces of our Passover puzzle are now in place. Where each had been part light, part shadow, this vagueness has now given way to a clear and brilliant vision of freedom, and a clear and brilliant vision of Jerusalem. With *nirtzah* we look neither to an ancient Jerusalem, nor to a Jerusalem of the distant future. With *nirtzah*—with *L'shana haba b'Yerushalayim*—we look to the imminence of Jerusalem, and the imminence of peace. We look to the Jerusalem that we hope and pray is just around the corner.

Way back at *urechatz*, we were transported to Jerusalem of old. It was then that we heard the words, "every goal must precede itself in thought." Jerusalem is our goal. Jerusalem is the only place where the wisdom and way of Jewish life can be fully actualized in a manner that liberates the potential of every Jew and of the Jewish nation to transform the landscape of history. Jerusalem is where the intimate relationship of the Jewish people with God can bear the fruits of a universal, spiritual symphony.

The fruit of freedom is peace—peace of mind, peace of body and soul, peace within us, and peace between us.

L'shana haba b'Yerushalayim. Next year in Jerusalem!

The Haggadah:
the all-time
Greatest Hits

5

The Haggadah is a fascinating text that can be carefully studied and contemplated for years without ever exhausting its vast reservoir of insight. On the night of the seder, the ideal is to read the entire text, and to share and discuss some of these insights. In this chapter, you will find eight brief excerpts, with accompanying reflections, from the most popular parts of the Haggadah.

The Haggadah is built around a question-and-answer format, and was structured this way in order to encourage inquiry and discussion. In keeping with that dynamic, many of our selections from the Haggadah will take the form of an excerpted textual quote followed by a question, and then a response.

Often, before the seder even begins, somebody asks the following question—

Question: I'm hungry, do we really have to read the whole Haggadah?

Response: The reading of the Haggadah is far more than the telling of a drawn-out, ethnic bedtime story. The reading of the Haggadah addresses itself to the innate human longing to know whence we come. A person is profoundly linked to his or her past, and a murky notion of one's origins can contribute to a sense of lonely detachment and inner estrangement. A child without roots is a child in search of place and purpose. Likewise, a people without a history is a people without a compass.

At the very least, the Passover seder confronts us with the responsibility of giving our children a sense of history—a sense of rootedness and belonging, of identity and direction. "This Haggadah," we need to tell our children, "this saga, is your saga. These events are your history, and these people are your people. The ideas and values contained in this Haggadah are yours to consider. They are your inheritance, your family fortune."

The Haggadah tells us—as we tell our children—"You are a Jew." This is your past, your present, and the essence of your destiny.

Matzah, the Bread of Affliction

At the beginning of the seder, when everyone is seated at the table, the matzah is covered. Then, the drama of the evening begins with the uncovering of the matzah and the reading of the following paragraph:

"This is the bread of affliction that our forefathers ate in the land of Egypt. All who are hungry—come and eat. All those in need—come and celebrate Passover. Now we are here; next year may we be in the Land of Israel. Now we are slaves; next year may we be free."

Question: Why did the Jews eat matzah in Egypt?

Response: Long before Manischewitz ever dreamt of egg, chocolate-covered, or whole-wheat matzah, our Egyptian oppressors forced us to subsist on matzah and little else. Matzah is more difficult to digest than bread, and though one may eat just a small quantity, the feeling of satiation lasts for a longer period of time. The compulsory diet of matzah enabled the Egyptians to reduce to a bare minimum the amount of wheat "wasted" on their slaves. The Egyptians also understood that a weakened body leads to a vulnerable spirit.

"All who are hungry—come and eat ..."

Once the matzah, symbol of our physical deprivation, is uncovered, we immediately turn our thoughts to the needs of others. The Pharaohs, Hitlers, and Arafats of history have made countless attempts to demoralize us by first crushing our bodies, hoping that our spirits would then be easy prey. Our enemies, however, consistently underestimate the depth and sensitivity of the Jewish spirit.

On the first night of Passover 2002, a Palestinian suicide terrorist walked into a hotel in Israel where scores of families were gathered to celebrate the seder. In an instant, an explosive, fiery, bloody hail of nails and screws killed twenty-nine people, and injured dozens more. Within days, the Israeli Defense Forces launched a large-scale attack on the terrorist stronghold town of Jenin. Had it so chosen, Israel could have easily killed hundreds of terrorists and destroyed their infrastructure by shelling the city from a safe distance, but it chose otherwise. Rather than risking injury to large numbers of civilians, Israel chose to put its own soldiers at great risk by sending them on the perilous mission of street-to-street and house-to-house searches for the terrorists. In general, this choice was a reflection of the Jewish spirit and its desire *not* to inflict harm if it is at all avoidable. The following story captures the spirit of one Jewish soldier who fought in Jenin.

Simcha Mellick is originally from Scotland and his wife Penina is from the United States. They both emigrated to Israel, and after Israel survived the Six Day War in 1967 the young idealists were married and helped build the Jewish town of Kiryat Arba near Hebron. Their oldest son, Gedalya, was born in Kiryat Arba. Later, the family moved to Jerusalem.

Gedalya grew up to be a passionate, religious Jew who was also a musician, a lover of nature, and a poet. At the age of twenty-one, he had also become a commander in the Golani Brigade of the Israeli Defense Forces. Gedalya was killed in Jenin and during the *shiva*—the traditional weeklong period of mourning—Gedalya's mother, Penina, spoke about her son's last days.

"In Jenin, Gedalya was carrying a chocolate cake that contained milk-based ingredients. He was saving the cake to share with his fellow officers. Gedalya's unit was there during the height of battle and fresh food supplies were not making their way to the soldiers. The men were looking forward to the cake, as their stomachs were still unsettled from having eaten little more than dry matzah. Gedalya cheered his friends by showing them the chocolate cake that he was saving. They had recently eaten some canned meat to lighten the loads they were carrying, and, in accordance with kosher dietary laws, they were waiting the three hours until it was permissible to eat a milk product.

"During this time, while searching a house, the soldiers found an Arab woman with several small children. The family became hysterical, they thought they would be shot on the spot. The soldiers spoke Arabic and asked the family to leave the house and walk to a nearby school where food and water were available. The family remained frozen in fear and couldn't move. Every wasted moment could have serious repercussions. Then Gedalya and his chocolate cake saved the day. Gedalya took out the cake and handed it to the mother. The woman stared at Gedalya in disbelief, and after a moment took the cake, gave some to each of her children, and then left the building for safety."

"The soldiers remained hungry for quite a while because heavy fire from terrorist hideouts made it impossible for supplies to be brought to them. Gedalya was killed in battle a short while later."

Gedalya Mellick died on Yom Hashoah, Holocaust Memorial Day, 2002.

All who are hungry, come and eat. As we have seen, the seder is about the birth of the Jewish people, and right from the outset we affirm our commitment to the maintenance of human dignity despite all efforts to denude our hearts of human sentiment and our souls of their inclination to share.

"All who are hungry—come and eat ..."

Question: *Now* we're inviting guests to the seder? How insincere can you get? The seder has already begun and there is no one around to invite!

Response: Clearly the invitation to "all who are hungry" cannot be addressed to potential guests. Rather, early in the seder, we lift our eyes from the Haggadah and address these words to those who are with us tonight. Sometimes, in our concern for people in far-off lands, we overlook the needs of those who are closest to us. At this point we reflect on our feelings for one another—for family and friends. It is time to let those who are right next to us know that their needs are important to us, too— that we are concerned, that we care, and that we will always be there for them. This point in the seder is a good time to think about what someone close to you needs, and how you can either assist or facilitate assistance. These needs can be physical, emotional, or spiritual.

"Now we are slaves; next year may we be free."

Question: What is meant by "now we are slaves"? In what way are we presently slaves?

Response: In a society in which freedom reigns and nothing is denied us, and in an era in which the click of a mouse can take us virtually anywhere we want to go, why do so many of us struggle to find our way? Why do we seem to achieve so little of what we truly desire? Why do so many of us cast about for a sense of accomplishment, of peace of mind, of fulfillment in life? Why is there such longing and groping, such squandered potential? Possibly, it's because we really are slaves, even in the midst of all our freedom.

A person without a goal is at risk of becoming a slave to the vision of others. So we must ask ourselves: What are our goals? We must determine to undertake the deceptively difficult task of reflecting, evaluating, assessing, and clarifying what it is we truly want in life, what kind of person we want to become, and where our deepest aspirations lie. Then, we need to realize that the price we must pay to actualize our goals and our dreams is the deliberate investment of immense effort.

Slavery comes in many forms and to live freely is a formidable challenge. A self-driven life is a long road strewn with potholes that masquerade as rest areas. Our world has gone from telephones to the Walkman, to fax machines, satellite dishes, e-mail, Palm Pilots, and soon to nanotechnology. All of these advances in capability and comfort are here to be used and enjoyed, but beware, for behind the luster of their user-friendly interfaces lurks the potential for ever more enslavement. The broader the range of possibilities in life, the greater the need to clarify exactly where it is we want to go. To know your goals and to set a course accordingly is the indispensable first step to freedom.

Mah Nishtana: The Four Questions

For many, the highlight of the seder is when the children have an opportunity to ask the famous, and timeless, four questions. Beyond setting the scene for priceless memories, the four questions serve as the entry point into the main body of the Haggadah. They are designed to initiate an animated process of question, answer and discussion.

The *Mah Nishtana* can actually be read in various ways. One can read it as four questions, as five questions, as one question with four examples, or as one question with four answers. In fact, at your seder, it might be interesting to ask people how many questions they see contained in the *Mah Nishtana*.

Regardless of how one understands the *Mah Nishtana*, it is clearly calling our attention to a unique night. A nighttime, a period of darkness unlike any other. And so we ask—*Mah Nishtana*—why *is* this night so very different?

I once drove with a friend from Cleveland to Denver. While driving, we not only encountered countless rest areas and a landscape dotted with Pizza Huts, Burger Kings, and KFCs, we also saw a land of spacious skies, amber waves of grain, and majestic mountains. Nightfall was approaching as we passed through the heart of Kansas, and within a few hours we were well into the Rocky Mountain state of Colorado. Denver was still quite a distance away, so we pulled off the darkened highway and slept by the side of a quiet road. With the sounds of morning and the first rays of sun, we awoke to behold an unforgettable sight. Only a few hours earlier this same world had been shrouded in darkness. Now, as if from nowhere, great snow-capped peaks pierced the clouds and surged toward the heavens. We sat there silently, awestruck by that moment of singular beauty.

There is so much darkness in life—dark, cavernous voids that gnaw away at us, darkness that clouds our vision of one another, our ability to touch, to communicate, and to love. Darkness that pits us one against the other—brother against brother, man against wife, and nation against nation. And in the dark of night, the Jewish nation was born. When the tenth plague, the plague that wiped out all firstborn Egyptian males, reached into the palace of Pharaoh and snatched his son, Pharaoh was finally vanquished, and in the middle of the night he proclaimed that the Jews were free to leave. That night, though surrounded by darkness, the Jewish nation could bask in the luminous rays of freedom.

Why is this night different?

Because on this night we experienced our freedom.

Why is this night different?

Because only on this holiday do all the special observances, the *mitzvot* (Divine spiritual directives), apply exclusively at night. On *Rosh Hashanah* we blow the *shofar* only during the day. On the holiday of *Sukkot* we eat in a *sukkah* during the day or night. Only on Passover do so many *mitzvot* apply only at night.

Why is this night different? Why is this the only night of the year so brimming with *mitzvot*? It is because, on the night of Passover, we not only commemorate the moment of our birth, but also express the very meaning of our existence as a people.

"I am God; I called you for righteousness...and I made
you a Covenant people, to be a light to the nations."

Isaiah 42:6

"For a mitzvah is like a candle and the Torah a light."

Proverbs 6:23

The purpose of Jewish existence is to be a source of light where otherwise darkness would hold sway. No matter how dark the world around us seems to grow, no matter how dim humankind's future may seem—the Jewish nation never gives up. Deep inside we all know that the world can be different. Deep inside we feel the call to cast a light on a darkened life or to illuminate a clouded corner of the globe.

At the foot of the Rockies, the night's cool darkness whispered to us, "There's nothing here." "Not so," said the light. "There is more than you can ever imagine."

Mah Nishtana, why is this night different? Because dark as our lives may seem, lost though the world may have become, we still believe in the power of light to illuminate our lives and our potential. We still believe in the power of light to be a radiant force for all mankind. The Jewish nation was born in the midst of a dark Egyptian night and imbued with a belief in the transformational power of light. This is the Jewish message, the Jewish mission, and the Jewish dream, and we will not rest until the dark night again shines like the day.

"And the night will shine like the day; [in the deepest
reality,] darkness and light are one."

Psalms 139:12

The *Mah Nishtana* is Answered

The Haggadah answers the question, "Why is this night different from all other nights?"—with a history lesson.

> "We were slaves to Pharaoh in Egypt, but then God took us out from there. [And when God rescued us from slavery, it felt as if] a mighty hand and an outstretched arm had reached out and saved us."

"We were slaves to Pharaoh in Egypt..."

Question: I'm sorry, but I have a hard time with a God who is strong enough to liberate the Jewish people from Egypt but allows them to become slaves in the first place.

Response: No victory is as sweet as that of the once-vanquished, no freedom as empowering as that of the captive, and no light as luminous as one born in darkness.

Without a doubt, no other people has endured what the Jewish people has been forced to endure. Yet, at the same time—

> *I will insist that the Jews have done more to civilize men than any other nation. They have influenced the affairs of mankind more, and more happily than any other nation, ancient or modern.*
>
> John Adams, second U.S. President

> *The Jews started it all—and by "it" I mean so many of the things we care about, the underlying values that make all of us, Jew and Gentile, believer and atheist, tick. Without the Jews, we would see the world through different eyes...think with a different mind...And we would set a different course for our lives. There is simply no one else remotely like them.*
>
> Thomas Cahill, *The Gifts of the Jews*

Think about it. When, somewhere in this war- and strife-torn world, sworn enemies extend their hands in search of peace, are they not reaching for that noblest of human ideals, an ideal originally expressed in the Jewish message to humanity that—

They shall beat their swords into plowshares, and their spears into pruning hooks; nation will not lift up sword against nation, and neither will they learn war anymore.

Isaiah 2:4

And yet, no other people has been so utterly despised.

Let us see what kind of peculiar creature the Jew is, which all the rulers and all the nations have together and separately abused and molested, oppressed and persecuted, trampled and butchered, burned and hanged [and now blown to bits by adolescent jihadists]. The Jew is the pioneer of liberty. The Jew is the pioneer of civilization. The Jew is the emblem of eternity.

Leo Nikolaeivich Tolstoy

On the one hand, Jewish history is a litany of mass abuse and human cruelty, while from another perspective—

Certainly the world without the Jews would have been a radically different place. Humanity might eventually have stumbled upon all the Jewish insights. But we cannot be sure. To them we owe the idea of equality before the law, both divine and human; of the sanctity of life and the dignity of the human person; of the individual conscience and so of personal redemption; of the collective conscience and so of social responsibility; of peace as an abstract ideal and love as the foundation of justice, and many other items which constitute the basic moral furniture of the human mind. Without the Jews it might have been a much emptier place.

Paul Johnson, *A History of the Jews*

Over 2,000 years ago, the prophet Isaiah anticipated the Jewish impact on civilization when he characterized the mandate of the Jewish people as being "a light unto the nations." The historical tapestry that is the odyssey of individuals, ideologies, and civilizations has but one constant—the Jew. Like the once mighty Soviet edifice of Marxism, the great empires of Persia, Rome, Great Britain and the Third Reich have all crumbled while the Jewish people looked on. Somehow, in some inexplicable way, a tiny and undeservedly maligned people has succeeded— like historical yeast—in becoming a primary civilizing agent for mankind. Those nations, those self-appointed chieftains of history, who would have eliminated the Jews, have unknowingly become disciples of the very object of their ire.

The great span of our historical lifetime is testimony to the fact that there exist no human or historical forces capable of overriding that which guarantees the seemingly impossible—the survival of the Jewish people. And the Jewish nation doesn't just survive; it thrives. To this very day, the Jewish people lives with honor, with dignity, and with a legacy of invaluable contributions to all humanity.

The Passover Haggadah is a portal to Jewish existential history, and the seder is a time when, as Jews, we confront our relationship to that history. Passover wants us to ponder this question: Was it worth it? Was all that our people has had to endure worth it, or would countless Jews—and the world—have been better off if we had exited the stage of history centuries ago? And the Haggadah wants to know what *you* think. Was it—or more accurately—*is* it worth the risk of being a Jew, of remaining a part of the Jewish people? When the seder night rolls around and your children ask that very question, you'd better have an answer.

Four Questions, One Answer, and Four Children

The word *Haggadah* means to "tell" or to "relate," and the key to a successful, meaningful seder is communication. In order to be able to "tell" the story of Passover effectively, in order to be able to communicate the meaning and relevance of Jewish identity in a compelling fashion, it is essential to know your audience.

"The Torah is speaking to four sons: one who is wise, one who is rebellious, one who is simple, and one who does not know how to ask."

With those four children, the Haggadah introduces the idea of four different types of people being addressed at the seder. Curiously, instead of just listing the four types, the Haggadah goes out of its way to emphasize the word *one*. *One* who is wise, *one* who is rebellious, and so on. We already know that the number four is significant on Passover, so there must be a reason why the word *one* appears four times in this paragraph.

By attaching the word *one* to each of the four types of children, the Haggadah insists that we focus on an aspect of parenting that Judaism sees as being of paramount importance. In the book of Proverbs, King Solomon advises us to "educate the child according to his path." This implies that each child, and every person, has his or her own peculiar and particular path in life; but it also means more. It means that the inner world of every child is unique and must be related to in a way that befits his or her character, personality, strengths, weaknesses, talents, circumstances and inclinations.

Passover is both the quintessential event for the transmission of Jewish identity from one generation to the next and a paradigm for the ongoing imperative of education, communication and transmission. As such, the Haggadah is highlighting the need to find that which is unique in every child—to identify it, nourish it, praise it, love it, and most of all speak to it. Our children are not mere replicas of ourselves, nor did they step off a page in the latest book on how to raise children. Moreover, there will never be another child who possesses the singular potential—the singular path—of each child that we have been entrusted to nurture and polish.

There is no better time to focus on your children and no better time for launching a Jewishly centered, tailor-made educational dialogue with your children than the seder night.

Jew Hatred

"And this is what has sustained our forefathers and us. For not only one has risen against us to destroy us, but in each and every generation they rise against us to annihilate us. But the Holy One, Blessed is He, rescues us from their hand."

Part I: The Lesson from Poland

During the summer of 1993, Steven Spielberg was on site in Poland filming *Schindler's List*. Today, compared to the over three million Jews who lived in Poland prior to World War II, a population of barely 10,000 remains. Given that the present population of Poland is 32 million, this means that in a Super Bowl crowd of 80,000 you would find about 25 Jews.

When members of Spielberg's cast and crew mixed with local Polish residents, they were shocked to find themselves confronted with open expressions of a visceral hatred for Jews. The Poles have taught us an astonishing fact—the fire of Jew hatred requires no fuel. Like some horrific alien, it is able to feed off its own flesh.

Teachers are experts at discerning the difference between excuses and reasons. Protestations of "but I left my assignment in my locker last night" often fall on deaf ears because, after all, couldn't a conscientious student easily have called a friend for the assignment? Thus, reasons are quickly unmasked for the hollow excuses they truly are. Consider the following list of ten reasons why non-Jews have hated Jews throughout history:

1. They are different from us.
2. They are becoming too much like us.
3. They are wealthy.
4. They are poor and parasitic.
5. They are not loyal citizens.
6. They are too involved in the government.
7. They kill non-Jewish children and use their blood in the baking of matzah.

8. They invented the God of moral conscience.

9. They killed God.

10. They want to rule the world.

Virtually every item on this list is contradicted by another. The question is this: Are there any legitimate reasons for Jew-hatred, or are there only excuses?

Part II: The Lesson From Israel

In 1895, Theodor Herzl, a Jewish journalist from Vienna, was sent to Paris to cover the biggest story of his day—the trial of a Jew by the name of Alfred Dreyfus. The Dreyfus trial was as big then as the Clinton impeachment trial was a century later. Herzl watched as the Dreyfus trial unleashed a torrent of anti-Jewish speeches, articles, rallies and sermons both in France—the heart of what he thought was enlightened Europe—and across the continent. Herzl, shocked by the depth of hatred he saw, became obsessed with finding a cure for anti-Semitism. The cure he proposed was the idea of a Jewish homeland.

To Herzl, because the Jewish people had no state of their own, they were doomed to always being history's "other"—a people whose only existential reality was that of the foreigner. Herzl's perception was that the roots of anti-Semitism lay in the fact that, as a stateless people, Jews would always be the eternal outsider, and as outsiders they would always be suspect, held in contempt, and despised. But a Jewish state could rectify this, and so by 1896 Herzl had written a small book that contained his prescription for anti-Semitism—it was entitled *The Jewish State*. Two years later, he convened the first Zionist congress, with the goal of establishing a Jewish state in the ancient Jewish homeland. The creation of a Jewish state would eliminate the fundamental difference between the Jews and all other people and thus eradicate the root cause of anti-Semitism.

Forty-five years after Herzl first dreamt of the creation of Israel, European doctors, teachers, farmers, politicians, peasants, merchants, maestros, lawyers, factory workers and professors enthusiastically joined the German effort to entirely exterminate the Jews of Europe. In the end, they failed, but they did manage to slaughter six million Jews, including one and a half million children. Then, not long after the crematoria of Europe stopped spewing out the ashes of Jews, the State of Israel was born.

In the aftermath of the Holocaust, though anti-Semitism became politically incorrect, it didn't take long for the world to find a way to couch its hatred of the Jewish people in more palatable terms. In 1975, the United Nations passed a resolution stating that "Zionism is Racism." The Reverend Dr. Martin Luther King astutely observed that, "When people criticize Zionists, they mean Jews. You're talking anti-Semitism."

In the world at the beginning of the twenty-first century, it isn't unusual to find newspapers in the Arab world reporting that Israelis are killing Arabs to use their blood in the preparation of holiday foods; European papers depicting the Jews of Israel as modern-day Christ killers; or political cartoons in the United States that compare Israelis to Nazis. In the summer of 2001, the UN convened an international conference on human rights in Durban, South Africa. At that conference, it was Israel, more than any other country in the world—more than North Korea, Iraq, Taliban-controlled Afghanistan, Syria or any others—that was vilified as the world's epicenter of human rights abuse. And in the post-9/11 Arab-Muslim world, many people genuinely believe that Israelis, in cahoots with the Jews of New York, were behind the attack on the World Trade Center.

Theodore Herzl died in 1904 at the age of forty-four. Had he lived another forty years, he would *not* have been shocked that the people of Europe were able to perpetrate the Holocaust, but if he were alive today he *would* be shocked that not only is anti-Semitism alive and well, but that the very country he envisioned as the antidote to anti-Semitism has in fact become the prime pretext for anti-Semitism. The cruel, historic irony is that if Herzl were alive today, his thinking and his search to put an end to anti-Semitism might lead him to conclude that the key to ending anti-Semitism would be the dismantling of the Jewish State of Israel. Instead, the more reasonable conclusion would be that, as long as there is a Jewish people, there will be forces that demonize us and seek our destruction.

Indeed, if history has taught the Jewish people anything it is that, *"for not only one has risen against us to destroy us, but in each and every generation they rise against us to annihilate us."* And, difficult though our history has been, it has also taught us that, *"...the Holy One, Blessed is He, rescues us from their hand."*

Jewish History—More than a Bedtime Story

"God brought us out of Egypt with a strong hand and with an outstretched arm, with great awe, with signs and with wonders." (Deuteronomy 26:8)

"With great awe—this alludes to the obvious fact of God's direct involvement, as it says, 'Has God ever attempted to take for Himself one nation from the midst of another nation by trials, signs and wonders, by war, with a strong hand, an outstretched arm and by awesome means; just like Hashem your God did for you in Egypt, before your very own eyes?'"

"One nation from the midst of another..."

These words are a quote from a section in the Torah (Deuteronomy 4:25-40), in which Moses delivered his farewell speech to the Jewish nation just prior to his death. Standing there, on the eve of his own death and of the Jewish people's entry into the promised land of Israel, Moses told of a future epoch of exile when "God will scatter you amongst the nations and you will be there a tiny minority." In his prophetic words, Moses went on to explain that one of the results of this long exile would be a tragic estrangement of Jews from God and Judaism. Moses foresaw a time when the Jewish people would seek meaning and spirituality in every sort of religion, ideology, and "ism" other than Judaism. Then, later in his address, Moses turned his vision, and his words, to the Jewish people living in that distant future. He knew that, having been set adrift on the rough waters of history, we would once again begin to seek the shelter of truth. But how would we know? How would we be able to tell if our very own Judaism contains an authentic path to achieving a bond with God?

To know this, Moses said, speaking to these searching Jews of the future, "Please investigate world history back to its earliest times and see if an event of this magnitude has ever taken place or if such an event has ever been heard of." And what is this unique historical event that Moses was referring to? "Has an entire nation ever heard God speak or has God ever brought one nation out from amidst another nation as God has done for you in Egypt?"

In quoting these words of Moses, the Haggadah gives us the essence of what makes the origins of Judaism unique. Judaism, and only Judaism, is rooted in a historical event experienced by an entire nation. The intellectual bedrock of Jewish belief doesn't rest on one person's claim to divinity or revelation, or that of a small band of witnesses. Jewish commitment to Judaism is ultimately rooted in the idea that, while national historical events may be open to reinterpretation, they can never be either fabricated or erased.

The Vietnam War, like the Kennedy assassination, will be debated for years to come. But there is one idea that will never take hold, namely, that these events never happened at all. No conspiracy theory is big enough to invent events of such national consequence in which so many people were involved. Similarly, though the leaders of the Soviet Union would paint Stalin in a variety of shades from savior to demon, they could never deny him or invent him. The national events that had Stalin at their helm were simply too big to hide and too far-reaching to be fabricated.

But Moses went even one step further. Consider his words carefully—"if an event of this magnitude has ever taken place or if such an event has ever been heard of."

Over 3,000 years ago, Moses predicted the unpredictable. When he prophesied that no such event would "ever be heard of," what he was saying was this: While the Jewish people will always stake its spiritual claim in the soil of historicity, no other people or religion will ever even attempt to do the same. And historical hindsight bears out this confident vision of Moses. For, in fact, no other religion has ever attempted to mount the stage of world history by staking its claim on the veracity of a national historic event.

And just how did Moses know that this would be the case? The answer is this: Though dreams, visions, and personal revelations can easily be claimed by any individual or committee seeking to found a religion, you just can't claim that a national historical event happened if it didn't. It just won't fly. Moses knew prophetically what logic likewise dictates. If the Jews were smart enough to come up with a story of national redemption and revelation, then eventually some other group would also invent its own equally compelling story. But we didn't, and they couldn't.

On the night of Passover, Jewish parents don't tell bedtime stories; they teach history.

The Ten Plagues

> *Blood—Fire—and Pillars of Smoke*
> *An alternative explanation of the preceding verse says that each phrase represents two plagues. Mighty hand—two; outstretched arm—two; great awe—two; signs—two; wonders—two. These correspond to the ten plagues that the Holy One, Blessed is He, brought upon the Egyptians in Egypt, namely:*
> *1. Blood 2. Frogs 3. Lice 4. Wild Beasts 5. Pestilence 6. Boils 7. Hail 8. Locusts 9. Darkness 10. Death of the firstborn.*

Pharaoh and the Ten Plagues: A Three-Part Story
Part I: Setting the Scene

Question: Why didn't Pharaoh and the Egyptians let the Jews go after one or two plagues?

Response: In the Torah, the story of the ten plagues is found in the book of Exodus, 7:8–12:33. There, the Torah reports that the Egyptian court magicians were able to duplicate the first two plagues. This convinced Pharaoh that he was dealing with a force he could contend with. However, classical commentators explain that a close reading of the text reveals that in truth the Egyptian magicians were no match for Moses and his brother Aaron. In fact, the best the Egyptians could do was to turn a small bottle of water into blood. They certainly couldn't transform the mighty Nile into a bloody waterway. Yet Pharaoh contented himself with these meager displays and continued to cling to his conviction not to free the Jews despite Moses' warning of even more dire consequences.

According to Jewish tradition, there is a little bit of Pharaoh in all of us.

Part II: Rationalization Reaches for Straws

Life is a battle. We all want to do what's right and good; we want to infuse our lives with meaning and spirituality; but it's such a struggle. Sometimes we are triumphant and other times, when locked in the pitched battle of life, we give in to our impulse toward rationalization. Rationalization offers us an island of respite as it enables us to justify actions that deep down we know are not for us. This remarkable ability, when viewed from a distance, might be laughable if it weren't so destructive. Like Pharaoh and his magicians, we often hang our hats on the flimsiest line of thinking in order to sanction choices that fly in the face of who we actually are and what we want to stand for. And if we are not vigilantly self-aware, then we run the risk of sharing Pharaoh's fate. In the grips of rationalization, Pharaoh the slave master became Pharaoh the enslaved. Clinging to straws, we often seek to excuse and justify our actions, while hurtling unchecked toward our own self-destruction.

Part III: The Tunnel Vision of Ego

You consider a course of action, carefully weigh all the options, and finally arrive at a conclusion. Then, having made your decision, you're off and running. At first the going is smooth, but soon you find that you keep stubbing a toe. Then you twist an ankle, injure a knee, throw out your back, and eventually run face-first into a wall that everyone saw but you.

Dazed and confused, you ponder a most ancient riddle: "Where did *that* come from?" The answer may well lie in the fact that the only thing harder than admitting you've made a mistake is running headlong into the consequences. Such was Pharaoh, and such is life.

Pharaoh knew that he was hopelessly outclassed and could never match Moses plague for plague. Nonetheless, he persisted even when persistence was senseless and futile.

To admit that the sum total of all our careful calculations and detailed planning is nothing more than a brilliantly charted course to failure is simply too much to bear. Our egos just won't allow us to hear of such nonsense. So we don a pair of designer blinders sporting the "Pharaoh" logo and rush off into the grasp of everything we wanted to avoid.

Or, unlike Pharaoh, we can choose to open our eyes and have the courage to sacrifice our egos before we sacrifice ourselves.

Dayenu—Enough

"The Omnipresent God has bestowed an abundance of favors upon us!"

"Had He brought us out of Egypt, but not executed judgments against the Egyptians, Dayenu—this would have been enough.

Had He executed judgments against them, but not upon their gods, Dayenu—this would have been enough.

Had He executed judgments against their gods, but not slain their firstborn, Dayenu—this would have been enough.

Had He slain the firstborn, but not given us their wealth, Dayenu—this would have been enough.

Had He given us their wealth, but not split the sea for us, Dayenu—this would have been enough....

...Had he brought us into the Land of Israel, but not built the Temple for us, Dayenu—this would have been enough."

Vision, Balance and Growth

The Jewish approach to living is growth-oriented. Judaism, like a loving if demanding parent, is forever encouraging us to go one step further—to transcend our present selves and to soar higher and higher. This outlook on life is the expression of an eternally optimistic and confident view of human beings. At the same time, this paradigm contains a treacherous pitfall. If the driving force in life is to continually grow, improve and better oneself, then this can tend to breed a concurrent feeling of inadequacy and even failure. What good, after all, are my accomplishments, if I can always—must always—be driven to surpass them?

It is to this dilemma that the two-sided coin of *Dayenu* directs our attention. In the first instance, *Dayenu* isolates each and every step from the redemption in Egypt until the Jewish people finally enter the land of Israel and build the Temple in Jerusalem. Here, *Dayenu* is suggesting that with each one of these progressive steps we stop and say, *enough*! Not that we lower our sights or rest on our laurels, but that we celebrate each particular accomplishment as an enriching experience worthy of standing on its own, and that with each significant step taken we allow ourselves to feel its inherent pleasure.

Yes, we can always deepen our relationship with God, but we must also know that each new level of depth forever changes who we are. True, we could always be kinder and more empathetic, but we need to be aware that every compassionate gesture makes an indelible impression on our soul and psyche. This is the view from the first half of *Dayenu*, and then comes the flip side.

The second half of *Dayenu* asks us to recognize that God was not satisfied with leaving us at any one of the stations of experiential growth, and that ultimately we had to travel the full distance from Egypt to Jerusalem. Therein lies a prescription for every one of us—to lift our eyes and gaze out at that which resides in the realm of the dreamer. As impossible as it was for the oppressed slave in Egypt to imagine the splendor of the

Temple in Jerusalem, as impossible as it was for a Polish Jew locked in a cattle-car bound for hell to envisage today's Israel, is how impossible it often seems that we will ever rise above our failings to realize our innermost dreams.

Dayenu—if our sights are always set on the most distant shore; *Dayenu* —if we relish every moment of growth; then *Dayenu* —there is no limit to what we can achieve and no end to the pleasure we will experience with each new stride we take.

Papers

6

Four Dimensions of Freedom

Every holiday has its own unique spiritual persona, and the persona of Passover is freedom. Each holiday's persona is revealed through the themes of the prayers that are particular to the holiday. As an example, let's look at the holiday of *Sukkot*. The main prayer for *Sukkot* refers to the holiday as *z'man simchateynu*, which means "the season of our joy." *Sukkot* is a festival that is particularly rife with opportunities to understand, experience and incorporate into one's being the quality of *simcha*, of joy.

Passover, on the other hand, is identified in our prayers as *z'man cheyrutaynu*, the "season of our freedom." On one level, this moniker is fairly self-explanatory, because Passover is about liberation from slavery. At the same time, on a deeper level, Passover is also about a different kind of liberation—inner, personal liberation. The existence of the holiday of Passover not only declares that Jews must regularly revisit the Jewish nation's experience of slavery and redemption but that as individuals we all need to periodically reflect on our own struggles with slavery and strivings for liberation. It is only the liberated Jew who is fully capable of expressing the dynamism of her essence. And only the liberated soul that can make her deepest impact on her people, and the world around her. The following are reflections on the theme of inner redemption.

1. FREEDOM AND SELF-AWARENESS

"I can do anything in the world I want. There is just one problem—I don't know what I want."

Question: Is this person free?
Answer: Yes and no.
Yes, she possesses the freedom to do whatever she wants, but then again no, for she is trapped by the stifling parameters of limited self-awareness. Though totally unrestrained from going any place at all, she is unable to take even the smallest step for lack of knowing where she wants to go.

✦ ✦ ✦ ✦ ✦

"Sometimes I get so frustrated. I know exactly what I want, but I still can't seem to achieve my goals. Halfway through one project my motivation wanes and I'm on to something else. I get distracted, caught up in other things—I just can't seem to stay focused."

Question: Is this person free?
Answer: Yes and no.
Yes, because he knows what he wants to accomplish and possesses the resources necessary for success, but then again no. For some reason he has become paralyzed by forces he seems unable to control. Is he afraid to take risks or is there an underlying lack of self-confidence? Is he still waiting for someone to take care of him or is he just plain lazy?
Yes, he is free, but he is unable to harness the inner capacity to actualize his freedom; sadly, he is also a slave.

✦ ✦ ✦ ✦ ✦

Now, here's the epitome of irony. The year is 1978, and a man named Yosef Mendelovich sits in a dank cell deep within the bowels of the Christopol Prison in the former Soviet Union. The date is April 12. On the Jewish calendar it is the 14th of *Nisan*, one day before the start of Passover.

Yosef is a prisoner. His crime is that he would like to learn more about his Jewish heritage, he would like to learn Hebrew and live a Jewish life, and he would like to emigrate to Israel. In the Soviet Union, all of these are grave offenses against the state. Yosef is a gaunt human shell and he is about to light a candle. Made of hoarded bits of string, pitiful droplets of oil, and stray slivers of wax, this is a candle fashioned by Yosef's own hands.

The candle is lit—the search for *chametz* begins.

Sometime earlier Yosef had complained of back problems. The infirmary in this hell provided him with mustard to serve as a therapeutic plaster. Unused then, this mustard would later reappear as *maror*—bitter herbs—at Yosef's seder table. A long-saved onion bulb in water had produced a humble bit of greenery. This would be his *karpas*. And the wine? Raisins were left to soak in an old jelly jar, water was occasionally added, and fermentation was prayed for. This was wine. The Haggadah that Yosef transcribed into a small notebook before being imprisoned had now been set to memory. The original was secretly passed on to another dangerous enemy of the state—Anatoly Scharansky.

Question: Is Yosef free?
Answer: Yes and no.

No, he cannot do whatever he wants. He has been denied even the liberty to know when the sun shines and the stars twinkle. For Yosef, the world of free men doesn't even begin to exist.

But then again yes. Yosef, perhaps, is more free even than his captors. Clearly self-aware, he knows exactly who he is and what he wants, and he is prepared to pay any price to have it. Today

---

*Today, after having served a long prison term, Anatoly Scharansky lives in Israel and uses his Hebrew name, Natan. Natan Scharansky is a prominent member of the Israeli government.

he walks the streets of Israel, studies Torah, and buys box after box of matzah to serve at his seder. He is a free man now, just as he was even behind those lifeless prison walls.

✦　✦　✦　✦　✦

Self-awareness means that we are able to stand outside of ourselves. In so doing, we are able to look within and, to a degree, assess the workings of our own interior world. How do we react to people and situations and why? When are we at ease, when are we tense, and when do we feel a sense of balance? What are our goals and priorities, and what are the values reflected in those goals? Are those values ours or are they someone else's? Where are we strong and where do we need to grow? What comes naturally and what requires great effort? Who do we love, what is it we love in them, and are we able to express that love? Are we being honest with ourselves, with others, and with God? Are we headed in the right direction? If not, why not, and if so, to what do we attribute our success?

Unaware of all these issues, we remain mired in a dense fog of confusion and doubt. Can we ever be fully self-aware? Probably not. Can we be aware enough to set ourselves free? Yes, and this is one of life's most pivotal challenges.

The achievement and maintenance of freedom is available only through this ongoing struggle for self-awareness. This process of clarification, coupled with the conviction to follow wherever it may lead, is the only way to achieve a spiritually sensitive, value-driven life of liberty. Ironically, this freedom can land you in a prison where you are the captor while your guards are the prisoners. Just ask Yosef Mendelovich—one of the freest people who ever walked this earth.

2. IDEALISM, CHAMETZ, AND FREEDOM

Idealism: More Than Kid Stuff

One day I walked into the high school classroom where I was teaching and was nearly tackled by a wide-eyed teenager supercharged with excitement. She could barely contain herself. "Rabbi Apisdorf, Rabbi Apisdorf!" she screeched, pleaded and politely demanded. "I have to show you something!"

Before I could even blink—much less respond—a newsletter from Amnesty International had been thrust to within an inch of my glasses.

April was a bright, energetic girl who was out to do no less than change the world she lives in. She was an adolescent mix of Mother Teresa and a rock-n-roll icon gyrating to benefit the latest victims of flooding in Bangladesh. And she meant it.

A few weeks after my encounter with April's membership in Amnesty International, I was duly informed that she was now a card-carrying member of Greenpeace. Before long she would be directing the school's Thanksgiving food drive, educating all who would listen about the plight of third-world babies, championing the cause of America's homeless, praying for an endangered species of rhinoceros, and graciously soliciting my sponsorship of bowling for AIDS—at ten cents a pin. I had no choice.

As time passed, April's infectious zeal began to stir some long dormant feelings, memories of what it felt like to believe that the world truly could, and in fact would, be a better place one day. As the school year drew to a close, I was almost convinced that once we unleashed April and her like-minded comrades on the world, by September we would surely return to a future in which universal peace and harmony were close at hand.

What about you? Do you remember what it was like to be idealistic? Do you recall how palpable and vigorous your convictions were? How doubtless your belief that if people would just sit down and talk with one another, reason with one another— love one another—that they would learn to transcend every artificially imposed barrier and find solutions to humankind's most daunting problems—problems of war, starvation, pollution and oppression, and all the other plagues of humankind?

Now ask yourself this: Was that really you, or was that just a naive and unseasoned version of your present grown-up self? Was there anything to that idealism, or was it just the immature folly and patently unrealistic dream stuff of youth?

How about this: Have you ever felt more free than when you were attuned to that part of you that said, "Somehow, someway, I know we can change this world." Deep down we all know that those rumblings, those dreams, that enthusiastically fresh idealism stemmed from a very real part of who we are. Deep within our souls we are all idealists.

When pondering the creation of the first human being, the Talmud asks the following question: "Why was the first human created alone?" To which it replies, "So that each person should say—the world was created for me." Far from justifying any and every abuse—"Hey, if it was created for me, I can do whatever I want with it!"—this supremely Jewish idea says, "It's your world and you're responsible for it!" There is a voice, a subtle yet persistent voice, that tells us all that we are here for a reason. It tells us that we can, and must, make a difference.

Scrubbing the Floors of Freedom

A funny thing happens on the way to Utopia. We grow up. We mature and learn that there is a "real world" out there, that we've got to be realistic, practical and pragmatic about life. We learn that little has changed over the millennia; that it's time we assumed some adult responsibilities; that the best we can hope for is to have a secure career, raise a nice family, perhaps make a contribution to our community, and then join our friends at the pool on Sunday.

This is what cleaning for Passover is all about. You see, as we abandon our dreams, we abandon ourselves. In the process, we consign our freedom to the trust of societal norms and thus we become enslaved. Slowly, without even noticing, we give up. We shelve our idealism and with it the hope of an empowered life of self-leadership—a life lived to its fullest.

This is not a suggestion to entirely reject everything the present "establishment" stands for; it is a plea for integration, for finding a way to reinstate confidence in our deepest potential—our Jewish potential—in the framework of the real world. Because when we surrender our souls to the comforts of convention, small cracks begin to appear in our hearts' resolve.

With time these cracks become gaping fissures of emptiness. The emptiness begs to be filled and this filler has a name. We call it *chametz*. (*See* page 20 for an explanation of chametz.)

Chametz is a great generic monster that grafts itself onto our being, insinuates itself into our consciousness, and becomes the focus of our thoughts, desires and life's activities. When we give up on idealism for the sake of monetary gain, we acquire *chametz*. When we squelch our search for achievements of enduring value and opt for the vicarious pleasure of watching others pursue victory, we acquire *chametz*. Whenever we settle for less and lose sight of what really matters, this, too, is *chametz*.

Chametz is bread, and matzah is a form of bread, but matzah isn't *chametz*. In essence, bread comes from the same simple mixture of flour and water that matzah comes from, only bread contains extra additives for taste and appearance and is also afforded time to rise—time to expand to the point where its potential to be matzah has become totally lost.

As Passover approaches, we rid our homes of the dough that became bread in favor of the dough that became matzah. Beyond seeking out the crumbs in our homes, our tradition urges us to also take a searing look within ourselves to see if we can't root out those insidious additives that have filled the cracks in our souls and commandeered the passion of our lives. When we divest ourselves of this presence, if only for a week, then what we will rediscover is our basic selves—our optimism, our idealism and our freedom. You guessed it—matzah!

3. Freedom, Free Will, and Responsibility

A Longing for Freedom

Of our myriad drives and desires, yearnings and inclinations, few are as passionate and compelling as the drive for freedom. Freedom is a state of mind. Even more, it is a state of being so essential to human existence that without it the fabric of our lives is bereft of quality, color, and texture.

Children instinctively chase a freedom that is as frightening as it is exciting. Youth defies authority at every turn to pursue the helter-skelter winds of freedom. They don't even know what they will do once they have it, but they know they must have their freedom. Adults, too, still yearning and longing, bolt the confines of career and family—all for freedom.

Thinkers from every discipline ponder and probe the meaning of freedom. Leaders call upon its power to inspire, and masses rise up to fight and die for it. And finally, there's America, that ennobled bearer of a torch held high to the huddled masses. At its idyllic best, it serves as a humble beacon for all humankind—the land of the free and the home of the brave.

What is Freedom?

Freedom is the capacity to express in one's life those values and ideals that stem from the essence of the human soul.

The Talmud says, "Precious is the human being who was created in the image of God." That all human beings are created in the image of God does not mean that there is a bit of Aphrodite and Adonis in all of us, but that we all have free will, and free will is a very precious gift. All human beings possess the ability to make meaningful and substantive choices that directly impact their lives as well as the lives of others. It is these choices that determine the ultimate moral and spiritual quality of every human being's existence.

Free Will and Responsibility

Everyone knows that people have the ability to make choices. If you ever did something wrong—and later regretted it—then you believe you had a choice. If you ever felt that a criminal deserved to be punished—despite the socioeconomic factors he was subjected to—then you believe in free will. If you believe that Raoul Wallenberg* was a noble and righteous human being, then it's because you believe that he made a choice where so many others failed. And if you ever yell at your kids for leaving their room a mess, then you most definitely believe in free

---

*Wallenberg, a Swedish diplomat during World War II, saved tens of thousands of Jews from the Germans.

will. You believe that people are not bound by the fatalistic chains of familial circumstance, socioeconomic condition, genes, or Divine predestination. Thus, if you feel indifferent, resigned and melancholy about life, you are a prisoner. Instead, you are animated by an abundantly optimistic outlook that sees yourself and others as shapers, creators and captains of great ships of potential.

You believe—as Judaism asserts—that people are people and not psychological robots, that the existence of free will automatically creates human responsibility, and that the most precious gift people can receive is the freedom to make their own choices and to be responsible for their own actions.

Avoiding Freedom

People shy away from choosing the freedom of being responsible for many reasons. Here we will address two of the most common: (1) The reason we don't effectively use our free will to live responsibly is because we never bother to clarify our core values and goals in life. This results in our being totally oblivious to some of our most critical personal choices, even when they stare us right in the face. (2) When we do achieve a degree of self-awareness and clarity, still we recoil at the painful prospect of exercising our free will, making tough choices, and assuming the full onus of responsibility.

Choice Management

Today it seems that business and the hyperspeed of technological advances are the metaphors for life. While there is something unsettling about seeing myself as a corporation, my mind as a software program, and my children as long-term investments, the fact is that the sages of the Talmud also viewed the workings of the business world as a useful paradigm for personal growth and character development.

The following model is designed to help you identify the values central to your life and then define a set of goals based on those values. Additionally, it will assist you in charting a realistic course for achieving your goals and sensitize you to the critical choices that you must confront in order to live responsibly and achieve true freedom.

This model is structured around a four-step process of introspection, projection and planning. It is straightforward, easy to use, and not set in stone. It is based on a Jewish discipline known as *cheshbon hanefesh*, personal choice management, and recognizes that ultimately people have to devise a customized approach that works best for them. It should be viewed as one way of doing things. The goal here is to provide a useful point of reference from which you can go on to develop your own personalized system.

STEP 1: *Make a list of five values or ideals that you want to express in the way you live your life.*

A partial list of desirable values and ideals:			
Accepting	Fulfilled	Kind	Resilient
Active	Gentle	Learner	Respectful
Appreciative	Giving	Listener	Responsible
Assertive	Go-getter	Loving	Self-aware
Balanced	Grateful	Making a	Self-motivated
Communicative	Growth-	difference	Sensitive
Compassionate	oriented	Mature	Sincere
Consistent	Happy	Modest	Spiritual
Contributing	Harmonious	Moral	Taking initiative
Daring	Helpful	Objective	Truth-seeking
Decisive	Honest	Open-minded	Understanding
Diligent	Humanitarian	Organized	Warm
Efficient	Humble	Patient	
Empowering	Humorous	Peace of mind	
Encouraging	Idealistic	Peaceful	
Energetic	Independent	Persevering	
Flexible	Industrious	Positive attitude	
Forgiving	Integrity	Positive	
Friendly	Joyful	influence	

STEP 2 *List five spheres of life in which you are most involved and/or in which you would like to qualitatively enhance your experience.*

A partial list of life spheres:		
Business	Friends	Personal growth
Career	God	Relatives
Children	Health	Self
Colleagues	Job	Spirituality
Community	Judaism	Strangers
Education	Marriage	Synagogue

STEP 3 (A) *Match a value/ideal to each of the five life spheres. This should be a value that you want to be ever present in that sphere of your life.*
(B) *Write a one-sentence statement that captures how your chosen value would be ideally expressed over the next ten years. This is your goal for that sphere of life.*

STEP 4 *List two or three concrete objectives that, if met, you believe will result in the achievement of the goal stated in Step 3.*

Examples:

1. Sphere of life: Marriage
   Value/Ideal: Loving
   Goal: Our relationship will be characterized by a continual deepening of our love.
   Objectives: (1) Twice a week, spend one hour of private time together. (2) Keep a list of "things I love" about my spouse next to my bed and add to it once a week. (3) Say "thank you" to my spouse at least once a day.

2. Sphere of life: Business
   Value/Ideal: Honest
   Goal: My reputation will be, "His word is as good as gold."
   Objectives: (1) Incorporate the following statement into my vocabulary: "If I make a commitment, I stand by it, so let me think about what we just said and I'll get back to you in an hour." (2) After describing a product or service to a customer or client, I will ask myself, "If I were my client, would I feel satisfied with this purchase?"

3. Sphere of life: Judaism
   Value/Ideal: Growth-oriented
   Goal: To possess the type of Jewish knowledge that enables me to be excited and inspired by my Judaism.
   Objectives: (1) Read at least four Jewish books a year. (2) Compile a list of my questions about Judaism, and ask a rabbi for answers.

When the Going Gets Tough

When one begins to see life as an ongoing process of making choices and accepting responsibility, then there is no escaping the reality that life is often tough. That's just the way it is. Embracing this fact is the first step in overcoming the hurdle of avoiding choices because of the pain involved.

The second step is to realize that it's a pleasure to be tough. We all know that the accomplishments that have most enriched our lives were only achieved because of the effort involved, the discomfort endured, and the difficult decisions that had to be made. This is a quid pro quo known to Judaism as "*L'fum tza'ara agra*," which means, "*according to the effort is the reward*." The reason mountain climbers aren't lowered to the summit by a helicopter is because the rewards—the satisfaction, pleasure, growth, thrill and sense of meaning—are all a direct result of the challenging climb. What's more, the climb itself is the pleasure. Being forced to abandon the imminent conquest of the summit of Everest by a sudden snowstorm will never engender regret in the heart of the climber because the reward *is* the effort.

Our tradition has it that only twenty percent of the Jewish people left Egypt. The other eighty percent died and were buried during the plague of darkness. Why did they die? Because they weren't prepared to make the choice of freedom. When push came to shove, they preferred the familiar routine of slavery to the unknown challenges of the desert.

Judaism says life is about choosing—choosing is difficult, yet life is a pleasure. This Passover, make a commitment to the pleasure of tough choices, and whatever you do—don't get left behind.

4. GOD AND FREEDOM: AN ODD COUPLE?

Let's face it, anyone who knows just a bit about Jewish history and a bit about the holiday cycle knows that, just seven weeks after being freed from bondage in Egypt, the Jewish nation stood at the foot of Mount Sinai.

When Moses petitioned Pharaoh in Egypt, he spoke in the name of God and said, "God has sent me to tell you, 'Let my people go, so that they may serve me in the desert.'" And sure enough, barely two months after leaving Egypt, there they were in the desert receiving not just ten, but six hundred and thirteen *mitzvot* (commandments). That's right. While everyone has heard of the famous Ten Commandments, most people don't realize that they are just ten out of a total of 613 commandments—248 positive commandments and 365 negative. And each of them involves dozens and dozens of details about how, when and where to carry out each individual command. So much for freedom!

Consider: A young prodigy enters the hallowed halls of Julliard School of Music. She is subjected to a grueling regimen of instruction and practice, followed by more instruction and more practice. Guided by the erudite vision and steady hand of a maestro, the student is carefully led through a progression conceived by masters. It is all part of the careful development of musical talent. The discipline is exacting, the demands are great, and the rules must be strictly followed. And the goal of all this is freedom—the nurtured freedom of spontaneous expressions of genius.

When watching a virtuoso perform, the untrained eye sees only the effortlessness of silken spontaneity. It all looks so easy, like Michael Jordan with a basketball. His movements are so smooth that kids everywhere think that all they need is the right pair of sneakers and they, too, will be able to perform airborne ballet steps with a basketball.

It's true that genius is a gift, but greatness is an achievement. All the God-given talents in the world will never budge from the realm of potential if they aren't harnessed, molded, developed and guided. This is exactly why masters, mentors and basketball coaches, though often rigid and demanding, are indispensable instruments of freedom. It is precisely their emphasis on discipline that unlocks potential, liberates talents and creates the dynamics necessary for the expression of seemingly effortless spontaneity and creativity.

Spirituality and Spontaneity

In the eyes of the Torah, every Jew is a spiritual prodigy. At the *Shabbat* meal on Friday night, Jewish parents bless their sons—"May you be like Ephraim and Menashe"—and their daughters—"May you be like Sarah, Rebecca, Rachel and Leah." Greatness of character, spirit, and moral fiber are the stuff every Jewish child is made of. In blessing our daughters to be like Sarah, we are not praying that they should become another Sarah— for there can never be another Sarah. Instead we pray that, just as Sarah's life was a remarkable expression of one woman's potential, such should be the destination of all our children. Our deepest hope is for them to invest their best efforts in an ennobled encounter with the special circumstances of their existence, nourishing the imaginable while making possible the unimaginable.

As Jews set out to confront life, it is with God as our coach and the *mitzvot* as a discipline of spiritual directives. This system of spiritual directives works to simultaneously harness and liberate the spontaneity of the human spirit in the dance of life. As detailed and far-reaching as the *mitzvot* may be, when set against the situational matrix of life, they are recast as indispensable signposts that hone our intuition as they indicate the direction in which we are to go, and grow.

The Torah says, "Be careful to observe the *mitzvot* of the Lord your God, and His ordinances, and His statutes, as He has commanded you. And you should do what is straight and good in the eyes of God." There is a perplexing side to this exhortation to carefully fulfill the commandments in the Torah. How could it be that after being told to "be careful to observe the *mitzvot*" that there is still room to say, "Do what is straight and good"? Are the qualities of straightness and goodness not requisite to a life of *mitzvah*-observance? Is a *mitzvah* still identifiable as a *mitzvah* if it is devious and corrupt? What the Torah is alluding to here is the fact that, even after one is committed to observing all 613 *mitzvot*, much in life is left unaddressed. In all those instances, be they interpersonal, professional, religious or otherwise, the Torah is saying that each individual must frequently be the arbiter of what is straight and good. The responsibility of living a life shaped by straightness and goodness is laid clearly at our doorstep. At the same time, we are not left directionless.

George Bernard Shaw said, "Only on paper has humanity yet achieved glory, beauty, truth, knowledge, virtue and abiding love." The *mitzvot* are études of character. On the surface they may appear to be a regimen of rote and ritual, but beneath the surface they have the ability to refine and mold the spirit. "On paper," every human being possesses almost limitless potential, and in practice it's *mitzvot* that guide us toward the fulfillment of that potential.

To think that it is easy to be a Jew because Jewish observance and practice dictate the course of one's every action is to be blind to the scope of each individual's potentialities; to the value, quality and sanctity inherent in every nuance of living, and to the presence of meaning in all encounters with things external to the self. From the straightness and goodness that animate the 613 overt *mitzvot*, we can infer countless other *mitzvah*-esque approaches to the ever-unfolding variables that real life calls upon us to address.

The Paradox of Commanded Freedom

The moment the Jewish people accepted the Torah from God at Mount Sinai, they became bound to its hundreds and hundreds of commandments, and all of its guidelines for living. What's more, our sages refer to the *mitzvot* as a "yoke," and to me the idea of wearing a yoke doesn't exactly jibe with freedom. The question is, "What happened to the freedom of the Exodus?"

The acceptance of the Torah by the Jewish people at Mount Sinai was not a repudiation of the freedom achieved at the Exodus. These were not slaves who sought to exchange one hopeless yoke for another. These were people who well understood that unharnessed potential is potential squandered, that an undirected life is a carelessly wasted life, and that the diminution of thoughtful rules and disciplines is an open invitation not to human freedom, but to savage chaos.

Johannes Brahms said, "Without craftsmanship, inspiration is a mere reed shaken in the wind." Similarly, the acceptance of the *mitzvot* was the acceptance of a system of spiritual techniques designed to educate and sensitize us to the qualities of straightness and goodness that are inherent everywhere in life. Still, even more than being carefully crafted means to a beautiful end, each *mitzvah* is also a deeply meaningful end in itself. In Jewish life, each *mitzvah* stands as an experiential moment of growth, insight and spiritual connectedness, while at the same time it lays the groundwork for the future realization of enormous potential. In this sense, *mitzvot* are commandments that liberate.

A Seder Full of *Mitzvot*, and Guaranteed Freedom

The seder night itself, perhaps more than any other night in Jewish life, represents the paradox—and the pleasure—of commanded freedom. As you know by now, the seder is chock-full of more *mitzvot* than any other holiday experience. For instance, at the seder one must eat matzah and drink four cups of wine (both while reclining), read the Haggadah, recite the verses of *Hallel*—praises, eat bitter herbs (without reclining), have a bitter herb and matzah sandwich, wash your hands twice (one time followed by a blessing and one time not), and lots, lots more.

I'll be honest with you. All of the *mitzvot* and all of the details that are required at a seder can seem a bit overwhelming, even daunting. Nonetheless, I absolutely, 100%, guaranteed-or-your-money-back assure you that, if you continue to invest time and effort in learning about the hows and whys of Passover, the seder will eventually become one of the most inspiring and liberating experiences in your life. It may take a year or two or three, but if you stick with it, you will find that within everything you *have* to do at the seder lie countless experiences that you will eventually *long* to do. I only hope that this small book has been a meaningful and enjoyable introduction to the wonderfully vast spiritual potential that is both Passover and Judaism.

L'shana haba ...

See you next year,

b'Yerushalayim ...

in Jerusalem!

epilogue

Steve wears a warm smile and sports stylish suspenders. His spry, robust gait and affable congeniality belie a fierce dedication to his roles as teacher, counselor, friend and jack-of-all-trades. Music was the passion of his youth. As an undergrad, he followed his heart toward music and social work. It was Segovia and Skinner, not Akiva and Hillel, who occupied his mind.

Eventually, one thing led to another and Steve became Rabbi Steve. For years he served as the Hillel director on a campus with a Jewish population of four thousand out of a student body of over fifty thousand. Come Passover, Rabbi Steve poured his heart into creating an enjoyable seder experience for his students. With over two hundred students present, the annual Hillel seder was a well-attended Jewish event.

One year a young man named Mitchell registered for the seder. His name was not a familiar one, and Rabbi Steve looked forward to meeting him.

Not long after the seder began, the rabbi felt a tap on his shoulder. In a perplexed and whispery voice, Mitchell asked, "What's going on here, and by the way, what are those books that everyone has been given?"

"This," Rabbi Steve began to patiently explain, "is a seder, and that book is a Haggadah. It is..." But before he could finish, Mitchell's voice broke in: "But where is the food?" And while the rabbi assured him that food would be coming, all his eloquent efforts at interesting Mitchell in joining the seder were to no avail. Mitchell already had plans for the evening. He had expected a seder like the one back home—a family dinner with matzah—not something that seemed more like Temple services than anything else. With that, Mitchell excused himself and left. And Rabbi Steve never saw him again.

As you know, the Haggadah speaks about four different children: one who is simple, one who is wise, one who is rebellious, and one who doesn't even know how to ask a question. Though the Haggadah refers to four children, there is actually a fifth. That child is Mitchell—the one who has other plans.

In many ways this book was written for Mitchell. Wherever he is today, I hope that somehow this book lands right in his lap. If you happen to know Mitchell—or someone like him—please do me a favor; lend him this book. And don't forget to tell him that he has an open invitation to the author's home for the seder.

ABOUT THE AUTHOR

Shimon Apisdorf is the educational director of the Jewish Literacy Foundation and an award-winning author whose books have been read by hundreds of thousands of people around the world. He has gained a world-wide reputation for his ability to extract the essence of classical Jewish wisdom and show how it can be relevant to issues facing the mind, heart and soul in today's world. Shimon grew up in Cleveland, Ohio, and studied at the University of Cincinnati, Telshe Yeshiva of Cleveland and the Aish HaTorah College of Jewish Studies in Jerusalem. He currently resides with his wife, Miriam, and their children in Baltimore. The Apisdorfs enjoy taking long walks, listening to the music of Sam Glaser and going to Orioles games.

Shimon can be reached at shimon@jewishliteracy.org

Did you enjoy this book?

Check out other titles in the JUDAISM IN A NUTSHELL series... a growing collection of books designed to make Judaism's most important ideas and issues accessible to people who are *long on curiosity but short on time.*

JUDAISM IN A NUTSHELL: GOD

JUDAISM IN A NUTSHELL: HOLIDAYS

JUDAISM IN A NUTSHELL: ISRAEL

You'll find these and other Shimon Apisdorf books at
www.judaicapress.com